GOVERNMENT PROCEDURES AND OPERATIONS

DELAY AND DISCRETION IN THE FEDERAL GOVERNMENT

BACKGROUND AND SELECTED ISSUES

GOVERNMENT PROCEDURES AND OPERATIONS

Additional books in this series can be found on Nova's website under the Series tab.

Additional e-books in this series can be found on Nova's website under the e-book tab.

GOVERNMENT PROCEDURES AND OPERATIONS

DELAY AND DISCRETION IN THE FEDERAL GOVERNMENT

BACKGROUND AND SELECTED ISSUES

CORY DERRICKS
EDITOR

nova publishers
New York

Library of Congress Cataloging-in-Publication Data

ISBN: 978-1-63463-482-3

Published by Nova Science Publishers, Inc. † New York

CONTENTS

PREFACE

This book discusses the general legal principles applied in determining whether administrative delays are reviewable in court in these two different contexts and then address whether the procedures outlined in the Administrative Procedure Act (APA) are applicable to these delays.

Chapter 1 - Congress regularly authorizes and requires administrative agencies to implement and enforce regulatory programs. As such, agencies routinely make decisions about when to promulgate regulations and when to enforce statutory requirements against parties who violate the law.

During the 113th Congress, the Obama Administration announced that certain federal agencies would not enforce specific aspects of the Affordable Care Act (ACA) for a period of time in order to allow the public to further prepare for proper compliance with the law in the future. This has led to numerous questions regarding how courts treat administrative delays of regulatory programs. When can a suit be brought to force the agency to apply the law?

It is important to distinguish between two distinct types of agency delays: (1) delays resulting from when an agency fails to meet a statutory deadline for promulgating rules or completing particular adjudications, and (2) affirmative decisions to withhold enforcement of a provision of law on the public at large. The former arises in a scenario in which Congress has enacted a statute that expressly requires an agency to take a specific action by a certain date that the agency fails to meet. Because agencies can often struggle to meet tight congressional deadlines imposed by laws, courts have established a balancing test, known as the TRAC test, to determine whether the agency should be compelled to take action. The second type of delay occurs in a scenario in which an agency refuses, for a period of time, to enforce a statutory prohibition or requirement that Congress has imposed on third parties. This type of delay is generally implemented by announcing a period of non-enforcement during which the agency will not pursue or punish non-compliance with the law. Courts determine whether these delays are reviewable in court by following the Supreme Court's holding in Heckler v. Chaney.

This report will discuss the general legal principles applied in determining whether administrative delays are reviewable in court in these two different contexts and then address whether the procedures outlined in the Administrative Procedure Act (APA) are applicable to these delays.

Chapter 2 - One common concern about federal agencies is the speed with which they are able to issue and implement regulations. Federal regulatory schemes can be quite complex, and establishing rules and completing adjudications can sometimes require substantial agency resources and significant amounts of time. However, critics point out that sometimes an agency can simply take too long to a complete task. Commentators and courts have noted that such agency delay can impact the effectiveness of a regulatory scheme. It can also impact regulated entities that must wait for final agency action. In some circumstances, a court may have to determine whether an agency has violated the law by unreasonable delay in taking action. Substantial case law has emerged for how courts will treat agency delay in a variety of circumstances.

Under the Administrative Procedure Act (APA), agency actions must be completed "within a reasonable time." Courts have jurisdiction under the APA to hear claims brought against an agency for unreasonable delay, and the APA provides that courts shall compel any action unreasonably delayed or unlawfully withheld.

When an agency has delayed, but does not have to act by any statutorily imposed deadline, courts are more deferential to the agency's priorities and are less willing to compel an agency to take action. However, if a delay becomes egregious, courts will compel an agency to take prompt action. Generally, courts follow the *TRAC* factors, from *Telecommunications Research & Action Center v. FCC*, to determine whether a delay is unreasonable. The court will see if Congress has established any indication for how quickly the agency should proceed; determine whether a danger to human health is implicated by the delay; consider the agency's competing priorities; evaluate the interests prejudiced by the delay; and determine whether the agency has treated the complaining party disparately from others. A court balances these *TRAC* factors to reach a conclusion on a case-by-case basis. It can be difficult to predict which way a court will decide any particular case. There is no strict rule on how long is too long to wait for an agency action. Therefore, it is important to look at previous cases to see what kinds of delays are determined to be unreasonable.

In addition to the APA's general requirement to act within a reasonable time, Congress may also establish specific deadlines for agency actions by statute. When an agency fails to meet a statutory deadline, courts generally compel the agency to take prompt action. Some courts have determined that a court has no choice but to compel agency action in the face of a missed statutory deadline. For these courts, no balancing is permitted when a deadline has been violated. However, other courts note that a statutory deadline is merely one of the factors to consider when determining whether the delay is unreasonable. For these courts, the *TRAC* factors are still evaluated to determine whether the court should compel the agency to act after a deadline has been missed.

Judicial remedies for delayed agency actions are somewhat limited. The Supreme Court has ruled that a court is permitted to compel an agency to take action, but cannot determine what conclusion the agency shall ultimately reach on the issue. Furthermore, the Supreme Court has also established that agency rules still maintain the force of law, even when they are promulgated after a statutory deadline. Therefore, a court's only remedy for unreasonable agency delay is essentially to impose a deadline on the agency.

Chapter 3 - The Take Care Clause would appear to stand for two, at times diametrically opposed propositions—one imposing a "duty" upon the President and the other viewing the Clause as a source of Presidential "power." Primarily, the Take Care Clause has been interpreted as placing an obligation on both the President and those under his supervision to comply with and execute clear statutory directives as enacted by Congress. However, the Supreme Court has also construed the Clause as ensuring Presidential control over the enforcement of federal law. As a result, courts generally will not review Presidential enforcement decisions, including the decision of whether to initiate a criminal prosecution or administrative enforcement action in response to a violation of federal law.

In situations where an agency refrains from bringing an enforcement action, courts have historically been cautious in reviewing the agency determination—generally holding that these nonenforcement decisions are "committed to agency discretion" and therefore not subject to judicial review under the Administrative Procedure Act. The seminal case on this topic is Heckler v. Chaney, in which the Supreme Court held that an "agency's decision not to take enforcement action should be presumed immune from judicial review."

However, the Court also clearly indicated that the presumption against judicial review of agency nonenforcement decisions may be overcome in a variety of specific situations. For example, a court may review an agency nonenforcement determination "where the substantive statute has provided guidelines for the agency to follow in exercising its enforcement powers," or where the agency has "'consciously and expressly adopted a general policy' that is so extreme as to amount to an abdication of its statutory responsibilities."

As such, it would appear that Congress may overcome the presumption of nonreviewability and restrict executive discretion through statute by expressly providing "meaningful standards" for the manner in which the agency may exercise its enforcement powers.

Nevertheless, legislation that can be characterized as significantly restricting the exercise of executive branch enforcement decisions, in either the criminal, civil, or administrative context, could raise questions under the separation of powers.

Chapter 4 - The two federal agencies primarily responsible for administering the private health insurance provisions in the Patient Protection and Affordable Care Act (ACA)—the Centers for Medicare & Medicaid Services (CMS) within the Department of Health and Human Services (HHS), and the Internal Revenue Service (IRS) within the Treasury Department—have taken certain actions to delay, extend, or otherwise modify the law's implementation.

Chapter 5 - The term *prosecutorial discretion* is commonly used to describe the wide latitude that prosecutors have in determining when, whom, how, and even whether to prosecute apparent violations of the law. The Immigration and Naturalization Service (INS) and, later, the Department of Homeland Security (DHS) and its components have historically described themselves as exercising prosecutorial discretion in immigration enforcement. Some commentators have recently challenged this characterization on the grounds that DHS enforces primarily civil violations, and some of its components cannot be said to engage in "law enforcement," as that term is conventionally understood. However, even agencies that do not prosecute or engage in law enforcement have been recognized as having discretion (sometimes referred to as *enforcement discretion*) in determining whether to enforce particular violations.

Federal regulation of immigration is commonly said to arise from various powers enumerated in the Constitution (e.g., naturalization, commerce), as well as the federal government's inherent power to control and conduct foreign relations. Some, although not all, of these powers belong exclusively to Congress, and courts have sometimes described Congress as having "plenary power" over immigration. However, few courts or commentators have addressed the separation of powers between Congress and the President in the field of immigration, and the executive has sometimes been said to share plenary power over immigration with Congress as one of the "political branches." Moreover, the authority to exercise prosecutorial or enforcement discretion has traditionally been understood to arise from the Constitution, not from any congressional delegation of power.

Certain decisions have been widely recognized as within the prosecutorial discretion of immigration officers. These include deciding whether to initiate removal proceedings and what charges to lodge against the respondent; canceling a Notice to Appear or other charging document before jurisdiction vests with an immigration judge; granting deferred action or extended voluntary departure to an alien otherwise subject to removal (deportation); appealing particular decisions or orders; and imposing fines for particular offenses, among other things. Enforcement priorities and resources, as well as humanitarian concerns, have typically played a role in determining whether to exercise discretion in individual cases. For example, the George W. Bush Administration temporarily suspended employer sanctions in areas affected by Hurricane Katrina, and the Obama Administration recently began granting deferred action to certain unauthorized aliens brought to the United States as children.

While the executive branch's prosecutorial or enforcement discretion is broad, it is not unfettered, and particular exercises of discretion could potentially be checked by the Constitution, statute, or agency directives. *Selective prosecution*, or prosecution based on race, religion, or the exercise of constitutional rights, is prohibited, although aliens generally cannot assert selective prosecution as a defense to removal. A policy of non-enforcement that amounts to an abdication of an agency's statutory responsibilities could potentially be said to violate the Take Care Clause. However, standing to challenge alleged violations of the Take Care Clause may be limited, and no court appears to have invalidated a policy of non-enforcement founded upon prosecutorial discretion on the grounds that the policy violated the Take Care Clause.

Non-enforcement of particular laws could also potentially be challenged under the Administrative Procedure Act if a statute provides specific guidelines for the agency to follow in exercising its enforcement powers. In addition, an agency could potentially be found to have constrained its own discretion, as some courts found that the INS had done in the 1970s with its operating instruction on deferred action.

In: Delay and Discretion … ISBN: 978-1-63463-482-3
Editor: Cory Derricks

Chapter 1

A PRIMER ON THE REVIEWABILITY OF AGENCY DELAY AND ENFORCEMENT DISCRETION*

Daniel T. Shedd and Todd Garvey

SUMMARY

Congress regularly authorizes and requires administrative agencies to implement and enforce regulatory programs. As such, agencies routinely make decisions about when to promulgate regulations and when to enforce statutory requirements against parties who violate the law.

During the 113th Congress, the Obama Administration announced that certain federal agencies would not enforce specific aspects of the Affordable Care Act (ACA) for a period of time in order to allow the public to further prepare for proper compliance with the law in the future. This has led to numerous questions regarding how courts treat administrative delays of regulatory programs. When can a suit be brought to force the agency to apply the law?

It is important to distinguish between two distinct types of agency delays: (1) delays resulting from when an agency fails to meet a statutory deadline for promulgating rules or completing particular adjudications, and (2) affirmative decisions to withhold enforcement of a provision of

* This is an edited, reformatted and augmented version of a Congressional Research Service publication R43710, prepared for Members and Committees of Congress dated September 4, 2014.

law on the public at large. The former arises in a scenario in which Congress has enacted a statute that expressly requires an agency to take a specific action by a certain date that the agency fails to meet. Because agencies can often struggle to meet tight congressional deadlines imposed by laws, courts have established a balancing test, known as the TRAC test, to determine whether the agency should be compelled to take action. The second type of delay occurs in a scenario in which an agency refuses, for a period of time, to enforce a statutory prohibition or requirement that Congress has imposed on third parties. This type of delay is generally implemented by announcing a period of non-enforcement during which the agency will not pursue or punish noncompliance with the law. Courts determine whether these delays are reviewable in court by following the Supreme Court's holding in Heckler v. Chaney.

This report will discuss the general legal principles applied in determining whether administrative delays are reviewable in court in these two different contexts and then address whether the procedures outlined in the Administrative Procedure Act (APA) are applicable to these delays.

INTRODUCTION

During the 113th Congress, the Obama Administration announced that certain federal agencies would not enforce specific aspects of the Affordable Care Act (ACA)[1] for a period of time in order to allow the public to further prepare for proper compliance with the law in the future.[2] This has led to numerous questions regarding how courts treat administrative delays of regulatory programs. This report will discuss the general legal principles applicable to judicial review of administrative delays in two different contexts: (1) delays in meeting a specific statutory deadline for implementing rules or completing particular adjudications, and (2) delays in the enforcement of a provision of law on the public at large. The report will then address whether the procedures outlined in the Administrative Procedure Act (APA) apply to these delays.

The first type of agency delay—delays in meeting a specific statutory deadline for implementing rules or completing particular adjudications—arises when Congress has enacted a statute that expressly requires an agency to take a specific action by a specific date. For example, the ACA includes a number of mandatory rulemaking provisions that require agencies to issue certain substantive rules by certain dates.[3] An agency's failure to meet this type of statutory deadline is generally assessed pursuant to a multi-factor balancing test established in *Telecommunications Research & Action Center v. FCC*, discussed further below.[4]

The second type of delay occurs when an agency delays the *enforcement* of a statutory prohibition or requirement that Congress has imposed on third parties. An agency generally implements this delay by announcing that, as an enforcement policy, the agency will not pursue or punish noncompliance with the law for a certain period of time. The underlying law takes legal effect and conduct in violation of that law remains unlawful, but the agency—in an exercise of its enforcement discretion—does not take action in response to violations of the provision until after a certain date. For example, although a provision in the ACA requiring that health plans meet certain minimum coverage requirements became effective in January 2014, the Center for Medicaid Services has announced that it will not enforce these requirements for certain plans for at least one year.[5] This type of enforcement delay would generally be assessed, if at all, pursuant to standards established for determining whether non-enforcement decisions are "committed to agency discretion by law" under the APA.[6] Given this framework, it would appear that the context in which an agency delay arises may alter the manner in which the court evaluates the delay. We now turn to the question of the legal standards to be applied in the two identified scenarios: where an agency delay has resulted in the failure to meet a statutory deadline, and where an agency is relying on enforcement discretion to delay the enforcement of a duly enacted law.

LEGAL STANDARDS AND LIMITATIONS APPLIED TO ADMINISTRATIVE DELAYS

Statutory Deadlines[7]

The APA does not provide concrete time limits for agency action—instead, it leaves most deadlines for Congress to establish, if at all, in the particular agency's enabling statute. Even absent a specific deadline, however, the APA states that an agency must "proceed to conclude a matter presented to it...within a reasonable time."[8] Further, section 706 of the APA states that courts shall "compel agency action unlawfully withheld or unreasonably delayed."[9] As such, the APA provides individuals with a cause of action when an agency takes an unreasonable amount of time to act.

However, a claim of unreasonable delay can only be brought against an agency for actions that the agency is legally obligated to take. The Supreme Court has stated that "a claim under § 706(1) [of the APA] can proceed only when a plaintiff asserts that an agency failed to take a *discrete* agency action that it is *required* to take."[10] If the decision to act is "committed to agency discretion by law," then no claim can be made against the agency for failing to take such an action.[11] In other words, an agency must be required to act by law in order to establish a claim that the agency has unreasonably delayed in acting.

Cases involving claims that an agency has unreasonably delayed taking required actions are typically brought when an agency has failed to meet a statutorily mandated deadline.[12] For example, if Congress requires an agency to promulgate rules by a certain date, or to complete adjudications within a specified period of time, a claimant may file suit against the agency for unreasonable delay if the statutory deadline has passed. Although courts generally are more willing to compel an agency to act if it has missed a statutory deadline, they will not necessarily do so. Instead, courts will often undertake a balancing test to determine whether the court should force the agency to act.

The balancing test commonly used by most federal courts is referred to as the *TRAC* factor test, after the case in which the test was first established, *Telecommunications Research & Action Center v. FCC* ("*TRAC*").[13] Under such an analysis, a court will assess whether Congress has established any indication for how quickly the agency should proceed; determine whether a danger to human health is implicated by the delay; consider the agency's competing priorities; evaluate the interests prejudiced by the delay; and determine whether the agency has treated any party less favorably than others.[14] A court balances these *TRAC* factors on a case-by-case basis to determine whether agency action should be compelled. It can be difficult to predict which way a court will decide any particular case as "[t]here is no per se rule as to how long is too long to wait for agency action."[15] Courts will often take a missed deadline into heavy consideration, but, generally, will still evaluate the remaining factors when determining the outcome of the case.[16]

If Congress is not satisfied with relying on judicial enforcement of statutory deadlines, Congress may insert "hammer" provisions into the text of certain statutes.[17] These provisions dictate what is to happen if a regulatory deadline is missed. The consequences for missing a deadline vary. Some laws establish a regulatory scheme that will be put in place if an agency misses a deadline;[18] while others mandate that the agency's *proposed* rule will go into effect if a final rule is not promulgated by the deadline.[19] Finally, at least one law has withheld funding from an agency until certain rules are promulgated.[20] Although these provisions can force an agency to act quickly, they can also be challenging for Congress to establish due to the extensive time that is often required to develop an effective regulatory scheme. In addition to these hammer provisions, Congress may always use political pressure, congressional hearings, and the appropriations process to influence agencies to act with more urgency.[21]

These types of administrative delay are relatively common as agencies may encounter difficulties in meeting statutory deadlines.[22] However, they differ fundamentally from situations where agencies use "administrative enforcement discretion" when deciding whether to enforce a statute or regulatory scheme.

Enforcement Discretion

When an agency decides not to enforce a statute against regulated parties for a certain period of time, courts are likely to review this as an act of enforcement discretion. Federal agencies generally have flexibility in determining whether and when to initiate an enforcement action against a third party for violations of a law the agency is charged with administering. This freedom in setting enforcement priorities, allocating resources, and making specific strategic enforcement decisions is commonly described as "administrative enforcement discretion" and arises principally from a combination of the President's constitutionally assigned obligation to "take care that the laws be faithfully executed," and the APA's command that courts avoid reviewing discretionary agency decisions.[23] Discretionary enforcement activities may include any range of actions, including, but not limited to, the imposition of penalties or the initiation of an agency investigation, prosecution, adjudication, lawsuit, or audit.

In situations where an agency *refrains* from bringing an enforcement action, Courts have historically been cautious in reviewing the agency determination—generally holding that such non-enforcement decisions are "committed to agency discretion" and therefore not subject to judicial review under the APA.[24] The seminal case on this topic is *Heckler v. Chaney*, a Supreme Court case in which death row inmates challenged the Food and Drug Administration's refusal to initiate an enforcement action to block the use of certain drugs in lethal injection.[25] In rejecting the challenge, the

Supreme Court held that "an agency's decision not to prosecute or enforce...is a decision generally committed to an agency's absolute discretion."[26] The Court noted that agency enforcement decisions, involve a "complicated balancing of a number of factors which are peculiarly within [the agency's] expertise" including,

> whether agency resources are best spent on this violation or another, whether the agency is likely to succeed if it acts, whether the particular enforcement action requested best fits the agency's overall policies, and, indeed, whether the agency has enough resources to undertake the action at all. An agency generally cannot act against each technical violation of the statute it is charged with enforcing.[27]

Agencies, the court reasoned, are "far better equipped" to evaluate "the many variables involved in the proper ordering of its priorities" than are the courts.[28] Consistent with this deferential view, the *Heckler* opinion proceeded to establish the standard for the reviewability of agency non-enforcement decisions, holding that an "agency's decision not to take enforcement action should be *presumed immune from judicial review*."[29]

However, the Court also clearly indicated that the presumption against judicial review of agency non-enforcement decisions may be overcome in certain situations.[30] The *Heckler* Court suggested that a court may review an agency enforcement determination "where the substantive statute has provided guidelines for the agency to follow in exercising its enforcement powers."[31] Additionally, the Court suggested that judicial review of non-enforcement may be appropriate when an agency has "consciously and expressly adopted a general policy that is so extreme as to amount to an abdication of its statutory responsibilities."[32] However, lower federal courts have only rarely had the opportunity to clarify these exceptions to *Heckler's* presumption of non-reviewability.[33]

It should be noted that dismissal of a challenge to an agency non-enforcement decision under the APA is not necessarily recognition by the court that the agency was acting within its authority. A legal distinction must be made between a decision in which a court reviews the merits of a challenge and approves of the agency action or inaction, and one in which a court dismisses the challenge for lack of jurisdiction before reviewing the merits. Although, as a practical matter, either decision results in the same outcome (i.e., the continuation of the agency decision), it would be inappropriate to state that a court that has dismissed a claim against an agency for lack of jurisdiction has accorded legal approval to the agency action or inaction.

Statutory Guidelines

The *Heckler* opinion specifically recognized Congress's authority to curtail an agency's ability to exercise enforcement discretion "either by setting substantive priorities, or by otherwise circumscribing an agency's power to discriminate among issues or cases it will pursue."[34] Congress may, for instance, choose to remove an agency's discretion by indicating "an intent to circumscribe agency enforcement discretion" and "provid[ing] meaningful standards for defining the limits of that discretion."[35] In this manner, Congress essentially overrides the inherent discretion possessed by the agencies in the enforcement of federal law and provides a reviewing court with a standard upon which to review the agency inaction. Although the exercise of agency discretion may therefore be influenced by congressional controls, it would appear that Congress's intent to curtail the agency enforcement discretion must be made explicit, as courts are hesitant to imply such limitations.[36]

In applying this standard, the *Heckler* Court held that the Food Drug and Cosmetic Act (FDCA) had not curtailed the FDA's discretion in a manner sufficient to allow the Court to review the agency's non-enforcement determination. The FDCA provided only that the Secretary was "authorized to conduct examinations and investigations" and not that he was required to do so.[37] Moreover, the Court determined that the FDCA's requirement that any person who violates the Act "shall be imprisoned...or fined," could *not* be read to mandate that the FDA initiate an enforcement action in response to every violation.[38] The FDCA's prohibition on certain conduct, although framed in mandatory terms, was insufficient to permit review of non-enforcement absent additional language delineating how and when the agency was to respond to violations. "The Act's enforcement provisions," held the Court, "thus commit complete discretion to the Secretary to decide how and when they should be exercised."[39]

However, in a pre-*Heckler* case, *Dunlop v. Bachowski*,[40] the Court found that a statute had removed agency discretion with regard to its enforcement in a particular circumstance. In *Dunlop*, a union member challenged the Secretary of Labor's refusal to bring an enforcement action to set aside a union election.[41] The Labor-Management Reporting and Disclosure Act (L-MRDA) provides that upon the filing of a complaint, "[t]he Secretary shall investigate such complaint and, if he finds probable cause to believe that a violation... has occurred...he shall...bring a civil action..."[42] The Court rejected the agency's argument that the Secretary's determination of whether to bring a civil action was an unreviewable exercise of administrative discretion. In doing so, the Court cited approvingly[43] to the appellate court's conclusion that:

> [T]he factors to be considered by the Secretary, however, are more limited and clearly defined: § 482(b) of the L-MRDA provides that after investigating a complaint, he must determine whether there is probable cause to believe that violations of § 481 have occurred affecting the outcome of the election. Where a complaint is meritorious ... the language and purpose of § 402(b) indicate that Congress intended the Secretary to file suit. Thus, [] the Secretary's decision whether to bring suit depends on a rather straightforward factual determination, and we see nothing in the nature of that task that places the Secretary's decision "beyond the judicial capacity to supervise.[44]

In *Heckler*, the Supreme Court confirmed the continued validity of the *Dunlop* decision, but distinguished the two decisions, holding that unlike the FDCA, the L-MRDA "quite clearly withdrew discretion from the agency and provided guidelines for exercise of its enforcement power."[45]

As discussed above, the language held to override the presumption against review of agency nonenforcement in *Dunlop* contained an express trigger for when enforcement was to take place. Federal statutes that do not contain language defining how and when the agency is to exercise its enforcement discretion, even when framed in mandatory terms, generally have not been held to override agency enforcement discretion. For example, a congressional command that an agency "shall enforce" a particular statute, without additional guidelines as to the circumstances under which enforcement is to occur, is generally insufficient to permit review of a non-enforcement decision.[46] The *Heckler* court suggested as much, noting that it could not "attribute such a sweeping meaning" to language that was commonly found in criminal provisions.[47]

Abdication of Statutory Responsibilities

In *Heckler*, the Supreme Court also suggested that the presumption against the review of nonenforcement may be overcome if the agency has "'consciously and expressly adopted a general policy' that is so extreme as to amount to an abdication of its statutory responsibilities."[48] The Court, however, was non-committal as to whether such an agency policy would in fact be reviewable, stating only that "[a]lthough we express no opinion on whether such decisions would be unreviewable under [the APA], we note that in those situations the statute conferring authority on the agency might indicate that such decisions were not "committed to agency discretion."[49]

In raising the "statutory abdication" argument, the Court cited to *Adams v. Richardson*, a decision from the United States Court of Appeals for the D.C. Circuit (D.C. Circuit).[50] *Adams* involved a challenge to the Secretary of Health, Education, and Welfare's (HEW) failure to enforce Title VI of the Civil Rights Act of 1964 (Title VI). The law in question "authorizes and directs" federal agencies to ensure that federal financial assistance is not provided to segregated educational institutions.[51] The Secretary asserted that the law provided federal agencies with "absolute discretion" with respect to whether to take action to cut off funding.[52] The court disagreed, holding—in language characteristic of the "statutory guidelines" exception— that "Title VI not only requires the agency to enforce the Act, but also sets forth specific enforcement procedures."[53] The court appeared to give great weight to the scope of the Secretary's non-enforcement, noting:

> More significantly, this suit is not brought to challenge HEW's decisions with regard to a few school districts in the course of a generally effective enforcement program. To the contrary, appellants allege that HEW has consciously and expressly adopted a general policy which is in effect an abdication of its statutory duty.[54]

The court determined that HEW had consistently and unsuccessfully relied on voluntary compliance as a means of enforcing Title VI without resorting to the more formal and effective enforcement procedures available to the agency. This "consistent failure" was a "dereliction of duty reviewable in the courts."[55]

Given the sparse case law associated with this exception, it is difficult to assess what level of nonenforcement constitutes an abdication of statutory responsibilities. It seems that if an agency announced that it would no longer enforce a provision of law against any individual at any time, regardless of the nature of the violation, a court could be willing to review the policy. Whether more limited non-enforcement policies— for instance if an agency announced that it will not enforce a particular provision against a particular group or that it will *delay* enforcement of a particular provision for a specified period of time—could also be subject to review would appear to be less clear. For example, in *Schering Corp. v. Heckler*, the D.C. Circuit held that the FDA decision not to pursue an enforcement action against a drug manufacturer for a specific period of time fell "squarely within the confines of [*Heckler*]" and was therefore not reviewable. [56]

It is clear, however, that announced agency policies of widespread non-enforcement are much more likely to satisfy the "statutory abdication" standard than more traditional, case-by-case, enforcement decisions. Indeed, in *Crowley Caribbean Transportation v. Pena*, the D.C. Circuit made a clear distinction between "single-shot non-enforcement decisions" on one hand, and "an agency's statement of a general enforcement policy" on the other.[57] The court determined that an agency's "general enforcement policy" was reviewable where the agency had (1) "expressed the policy as a formal regulation"; (2) "articulated [the policy] in some form of universal policy statement"; or (3) otherwise "[laid] out a general policy delineating the boundary between enforcement and non-enforcement" that "purport[s] to speak to a broad class of parties."[58] The court articulated its reasons for finding review of general enforcement policies to be appropriate as follows:

> By definition, expressions of broad enforcement policies are abstracted from the particular combinations of facts the agency would encounter in individual enforcement proceedings. As general statements, they are more likely to be direct interpretations of the commands of the substantive statute rather than the sort of mingled assessments of fact, policy, and law that drive an individual enforcement decision and that are, as *Chaney* recognizes, peculiarly within the agency's expertise and discretion. Second, an agency's pronouncement of a broad policy against enforcement poses special risks that it "has consciously and expressly adopted a general policy that is so extreme as to amount to an abdication of its statutory responsibilities," a situation in which the normal presumption of non-reviewability may be inappropriate. Finally, an agency will generally present a clearer (and more easily reviewable) statement of its reasons for acting when formally articulating a broadly applicable enforcement policy, whereas such statements in the context of individual decisions to forego enforcement tend to be cursory, ad hoc, or post hoc.[59]

PROCEDURAL REQUIREMENTS FOR IMPLEMENTING A DELAY

Whether an agency must follow notice and comment rulemaking procedures when it declares its intent to delay enforcement of certain provisions of a statute depends on whether the declaration is considered a "rule" for the purposes of section 553 of the APA. Only "legislative rules" are subject to the informal rulemaking procedures outlined in the APA; an agency may promulgate guidance documents and interpretive rules without having to undergo notice and comment procedures.[60] A party may challenge an agency's characterization of any action and argue that a particular statement should have been issued pursuant to notice and comment procedures.[61] However, courts sometimes have difficulty differentiating between general statements of policy, such as guidance documents, and legislative rules.[62]

Courts have described a legislative rule to be a rule through which an agency "intends to create a new law, rights or duties," or a rule that is "issued by an agency pursuant to statutory authority and which implement[s] the statute."[63] Similarly, one court explained that a rule is legislative if "in the absence of the rule there would not be an adequate legislative basis for enforcement action or other agency action to confer benefits or ensure the performance of duties."[64] Notably, courts distinguish legislative rules from guidance documents because they have a binding effect: "[I]f a statement has a present-day binding effect, it is legislative."[65]

Guidance documents, which are not defined by the APA, generally are considered to be a particular type of agency rule, known as a "general statement of policy."[66] The APA provides that an agency may issue these general statements of policy without having to undergo notice and comment rulemaking procedures.[67] According to the Office of Management and Budget's (OMB) Final Bulletin on Agency Good Guidance Practices, the term "guidance document" is defined as "an agency statement of general applicability and future effect, other than a regulatory action ... that sets forth a policy on a statutory, regulatory or technical issue or an interpretation of a statutory or regulatory issue."[68] Similarly, the Supreme Court has defined the term "general statement of policy" to be a statement "issued by an agency to advise the public prospectively of the manner in which the agency proposes to exercise a discretionary power."[69] Therefore, guidance documents do not create new legal obligations on the public, but, instead, inform the public on how an agency intends to carry out certain agency functions. One court notes that a statement cannot be characterized as a guidance document, and is instead a legislative rule, if the pronouncement "narrowly limits administrative discretion or establishes a binding norm."

Although it can be difficult to ascertain whether a court would characterize an agency statement delaying enforcement actions as a guidance document or a legislative rule, the following examples of such agency statements may provide some guidance on this issue.[70]

Exercising Enforcement Discretion

It appears that, at least in some circumstances, a statement addressing agency enforcement priorities could qualify as a guidance document. When an agency declares that it will only enforce a particular law at a certain time or under certain circumstances, it is not imposing a new legal obligation on the public. In fact, the underlying legal obligation technically remains in effect. Instead, the agency has simply informed the public that it will not seek to enforce the provisions of the statute in the enumerated situations.[71] As addressed in *Heckler*, it seems the agency could be viewed as exercising administrative discretion when it determines that enforcement of the law in a particular situation should not proceed.[72] Because an agency's decision to enforce a statute in a given situation is discretionary,[73] an agency's announcement of its enforcement policy would appear to qualify as a guidance document under the Supreme Court's decision in *Lincoln v. Vigil*, which describes a general statement of policy as a statement "issued by an agency to advise the public prospectively of the manner in which the agency proposes to exercise a discretionary power."[74] Further, because such a declaration would not appear to impose any new legal obligations on the public, it would seem that a court could determine that such a statement would not require notice and comment procedures prior to promulgation.[75]

For example, on July 3, 2013, the Internal Revenue Service (IRS) issued Notice 2013-45 (Notice), stating that the IRS would not enforce the "employer mandate" of the ACA during 2014 in order to allow for "additional time for input from employers" on how the law can be effectively implemented.[76] The Notice further encourages employers to "voluntarily comply with the information reporting provisions."[77] The IRS promulgated the Notice without undergoing notice and comment rulemaking procedures. However, the IRS does not appear to impose a new legal obligation on any parties, but, rather, the IRS seems to notify the public of its intent to not enforce these provisions against employers during 2014.[78] A court would likely find that such a statement is a guidance document, because it merely notifies the public on how the agency plans to perform a discretionary function—enforcement discretion.[79]

However, in other circumstances, an agency's declaration of a delay or enforcement policy could require notice and comment procedures. In February 2014, the IRS announced final regulations implementing the employer mandate from the Affordable Care Act.[80] In those regulations, the IRS provided for "transition relief" from the employer mandate tax for certain employers—that is, qualifying employers would not have to pay the tax.[81] In order to be eligible for transition relief, employers must certify that they have met certain requirements established by the agency.[82] Here, because the IRS is *requiring* employers to conduct a specific activity in order to be eligible for the transition relief—that is, provide certification—the transition relief is imposing a legal obligation on a party in order to qualify for a specific form of tax treatment. It would appear that an agency taking this approach to delaying a statutory provision would have to use informal rulemaking procedures because the agency would impose a legal obligation on a party, who wanted to benefit from the delay.[83]

Missing Statutory Deadlines

Under the other form of agency delay—that is, where an agency fails to take a discrete action by a statutory deadline—no rulemaking is required. Often the agency has simply not been able to accomplish the required action within the time provided by Congress. In this type of situation, the agency has not taken any action; therefore, no rulemaking procedures are required. However, as mentioned above, an agency may be subject to a suit by a party seeking to compel the agency to take action.[84]

End Notes

[1] P.L. 111-148 (2010). ACA was amended by the Health Care Education and Reconciliation Act of 2010, P.L. 111-152 (2010) (HCERA). These Acts will be collectively referred to in this memorandum as "ACA."

[2] See Internal Revenue Service, Notice 2013-45, NOT-129718-13 (July 3, 2013), available at http://www.irs.gov/pub/irs-drop/n-13-45.PDF.

[3] For example, section 6001(a) of the ACA requires the Secretary of HHS to issue rules relating to physician ownership and investment in hospitals by January 1, 2012. These regulations were issued on November 30, 2011. 76 FR 74122. For a general discussion of mandatory and discretionary rules issued under the ACA see CRS Report R43386, Upcoming Rules Pursuant to the Patient Protection and Affordable Care Act: The Fall 2013 Unified Agenda, by Maeve P. Carey and Michelle D. Christensen.

[4] 750 F.2d 70 (D.C. Cir. 1984).

[5] For a discussion of this delay see, CRS Report WSLG724, Obama Administration's "Fix" for Insurance Cancellations: A Legal Overview, by Jennifer A. Staman, Todd Garvey, and Daniel T. Shedd.

[6] 5 U.S.C. § 701(a); see also Heckler v. Chaney, 470 U.S. 821 (1985).

[7] For additional information on how courts treat claims of unreasonable delay under the APA, see CRS Report R43013, Administrative Agencies and Claims of Unreasonable Delay: Analysis of Court Treatment, by Daniel T. Shedd.

[8] 5 U.S.C. § 555(b).

[9] Id. at § 706(1).

[10] Norton v. Southern Utah Wilderness Alliance, 542 U.S. 55, 64 (2004) (emphasis in original).

[11] 5 U.S.C. § 701(a)(1), (2).

[12] See, e.g., Biodiversity Legal Foundation v. Badgley, 309 F.3d 1166 (9th Cir. 2002); In re Blue Water Network and Ocean Advocates, 234 F.3d 1305 (D.C. Cir. 2000); In Re Barr Laboratories, Inc., 930 F.2d 72 (D.C. Cir. 1991).

[13] 750 F.2d 70 (D.C. Cir. 1984) ("TRAC").

[14] Id. at 80 (internal quotations omitted).

[15] In re Barr Laboratories, Inc., 930 F.2d 72, 76 (D.C. Cir. 1991).

[16] See In re Blue Water Network and Ocean Advocates, 234 F.3d 1305 (D.C. Cir. 2000) (applying the TRAC factors to determine whether to compel an agency to act even though it missed a statutory deadline by a margin of 8 years); In Re Barr Laboratories, Inc., 930 F.2d 72 (D.C. Cir. 1991) (applying the TRAC factors and then concluding: "Though we agree with Barr that FDA's sluggish pace violates a statutory deadline, we conclude that this is not an appropriate case for equitable relief."); but, see Forrest Guardians v. Babbitt, 174 F.3d 1178 (10th Cir. 1998) (holding that when an agency fails to act by a "statutorily imposed absolute deadline," the action has been "unlawfully withheld" and the court has no choice but to compel the agency to act). It is worth noting that if an agency promulgates a rule after the statutory deadline for issuing such a rule has passed, the delayed regulation would still be valid, unless the underlying statute provides otherwise. Barnhart v. Peabody Coal Co., 537 U.S. 149, 155, 171-72 (2003).

[17] See Jeffrey S. Lubbers, A Guide to Federal Agency Rulemaking 15–16 (4th ed. 2006).

[18] See, e.g., 42 U.S.C. § 6924(d)(1-2).

[19] See, e.g., The Nutrition Labeling and Education Act of 1990, P.L. 101-535.

[20] See Department of Transportation and Related Agencies Appropriations Act, 1988, P.L. 100-202, Title 1.

[21] For more information on the congressional oversight process, see CRS Report RL30240, Congressional Oversight Manual, by Todd Garvey et al. For more information on controlling agencies through appropriation, see CRS Legal Sidebar WSLG789, 2014 Omnibus Appropriations: Controlling Federal Agencies through Appropriations, by Daniel T. Shedd.

[22] See, e.g., Biodiversity Legal Foundation v. Badgley, 309 F.3d 1166 (9th Cir. 2002); In re Blue Water Network and Ocean Advocates, 234 F.3d 1305 (D.C. Cir. 2000); In Re Barr Laboratories, Inc., 930 F.2d 72 (D.C. Cir. 1991).

[23] See Heckler v. Chaney, 470 U.S. 821, 832 (1985) ("[W]e recognize that an agency's refusal to institute proceedings shares to some extent the characteristics of the decision of a prosecutor in the Executive Branch not to indict — a decision which has long been regarded as the special province of the Executive Branch, inasmuch as it is the Executive who is charged by the Constitution to 'take Care that the Laws be faithfully executed.'"). It would appear that agency enforcement discretion exercised in the administrative context, though similar, is to be distinguished from prosecutorial discretion exercised in the criminal context.

[24] Under the APA all final agency actions are presumptively reviewable by a federal court. See 5 U.S.C. §§ 701, 702, 704. However, the APA excludes from review "agency action committed to agency discretion by law." 5 U.S.C. § 701; See also Citizens to Preserve

Overton Park, Inc. v. Volpe, 401 U.S. 402, 410 (1971) (holding that the "committed to agency discretion" exception to judicial review is "very narrow" and "is applicable in those rare instances where 'statutes are drawn in such broad terms that in a given case there is no law to apply'") (citing S. Rep. No. 752, 79th Cong., 1st Sess., 26 (1945)).

[25] 470 U.S. 821.

[26] Id. at 831.

[27] Id.

[28] Id. at 831-32.

[29] Id. at 832.

[30] For example, enforcement decisions must not be carried out in a discriminatory manner such that the agency is in violation of the Equal Protection Clause. Yick Wo v. Hopkins 118 U.S. 356 (1886). The D.C Circuit has also held that the Heckler presumption does not apply when a non-enforcement decision is actually an agency interpretation of a statute. See Edison Elec. Inst. v. EPA, 996 F.2d 326, 333 (D.C. Cir. 1993) ("'[N]othing in the holding or policy of Heckler v. Chaney [] precludes review of a ...challenge of an agency's announcement of its interpretation of a statute,' even when that interpretation is advanced in the context of a decision not to take enforcement action.") (citations omitted). This report briefly focuses on only two exceptions.

[31] Heckler, 470 U.S. at 832.

[32] Id. at 833 n.4.

[33] The dearth of case law relating to agency non-enforcement may be due to the difficulty of finding a plaintiff who has been sufficiently injured by agency inaction to obtain standing. See, e.g., CRS Legal Sidebar, Obama Administration Delays Implementation of ACA's Employer Responsibility Requirements: A Brief Legal Overview.

[34] Heckler, 470 U.S. at 833. See also Souder v. Brennan, 367 F. Supp. 808, 811-12 (D.D.C. 1973) ("It is undisputed that the Department of Labor has a declared policy of non-enforcement of the minimum wage and overtime provisions with regard to patient-workers at non-Federal institutions for the mentally-ill. It is also clear to the Court that if the Fair Labor Standards Act does apply to such patient-workers then the policy of non-enforcement is a violation of the Secretary's duty to enforce the law.").

[35] Heckler, 470 U.S. at 834.

[36] The D.C. Circuit has suggested that "guidelines" can take the form of "standards in the statute itself, in regulations promulgated by an administrative agency in carrying out its statutory mandate, or in other binding expressions of agency viewpoint." Crowley Caribbean Transp. v. Pena, 37 F.3d 671, 677 (D.C. Cir. 1994) (citations omitted).

[37] 21 U.S.C. § 372.

[38] Heckler, 470 U.S. at 835.

[39] Id.

[40] 421 U.S. 560 (1975).

[41] Id.

[42] 29 U.S.C. § 482.

[43] Dunlop v. Bachowski, 421 U.S. 560, 567 n.7 (1975) ("We agree with the Court of Appeals, for the reasons stated in its opinion, 502 F. 2d 79, 86-88 (CA3 1974), that there is no merit in the Secretary's contention that his decision is an unreviewable exercise of prosecutorial discretion.").

[44] Bachowski v. Brennan, 502 F.2d 79, 88 (3rd Cir. 1974).

[45] Heckler, 470 U.S. at 834.

[46] See, e.g., id. at 835 ("The section on criminal sanctions states baldly that any person who violates the Act's substantive prohibitions 'shall be imprisoned. . . or fined.' Respondents argue that this statement mandates criminal prosecution of every violator of the Act but they adduce no indication in case law or legislative history that such was Congress' intention in using this language, which is commonly found in the criminal provisions of Title 18 of the United States Code. See, e.g., 18 U.S.C. § 471 (counterfeiting); 18 U.S.C. § 1001 (false statements to Government officials); 18 U.S.C. § 1341 (mail fraud). We are unwilling to attribute such a sweeping meaning to this language...").

[47] Id.; see also Atlantic Green Sea Turtle v. County Council of Volusia County, 2005 U.S. Dist. LEXIS 38841 (2005) (holding that just because the Endangered Species Act said that violations of regulations "shall" be enforced, the statute did not remove agency enforcement discretion).

[48] Heckler, 470 U.S. at 833 n.4 (citing Adams v. Richardson, 480 F.2d 1159 (D.C. Cir. 1973).

[49] Id.

[50] 480 F.2d 1159 (1973).

[51] 42 U.S.C. § 2000d-1.

[52] Adams, 480 F.2d at 1162.

[53] Id.

[54] Id. The court also noted that HEW was playing an affirmative role in the violation of federal law by "actively supplying segregated institutions with federal funds." Id. The court acknowledged that it is one thing to say the agency "lacks the resources necessary to locate and prosecute every civil rights violator" and "quite another to say HEW may affirmatively continue to channel federal funds to defaulting schools." Id.

[55] Id. at 1163.

[56] 779 F.2d 683, 685 (D.C. Cir. 1985). The agency had bound itself not to initiate an enforcement action by the terms of a settlement agreement.

[57] 37 F.3d 671, 676 (D.C. Cir. 1994).

[58] Id. at 676-77.

[59] Id. at 677 (citations omitted).

[60] 5 U.S.C. § 553.

[61] 5 U.S.C. § 706(2)(D).

[62] See Community Nutrition Institute v. Young, 818 F.2d 943, 946 (D.C. Cir. 1987) (citing cases and articles that describe the distinction as "fuzzy," "blurred," and "enshrouded in considerable smog"); Hoctor v. United States Dep't of Agriculture, 82 F.3d 165, 167 (7th Cir. 1996); JEFFREY S. LUBBERS, A GUIDE TO FEDERAL AGENCY RULEMAKING 75 (4th ed. 2006).

[63] General Motors Corp. v. Ruckelshaus, 742 F.2d 1561, 1565 (D.C. Cir. 1984) (en banc); TOM C. CLARK, ATTORNEY GENERAL, ATTORNEY GENERAL'S MANUAL ON THE ADMINISTRATIVE PROCEDURE ACT 30 n.3 (1947), available at http://www.law.fsu.edu/library/admin/1947iii.html.

[64] American Mining Congress v. Mine Safety & Health Administration, 995 F.2d 1106, 1112 (D.C. Cir. 1993).

[65] Community Nutrition Institute v. Young, 818 F.2d 943, 946 n. 4 (D.C. Cir. 1987).

[66] 5 U.S.C. § 553(d)(3)(A).

[67] Id.

[68] Office of Management and Budget, Final Bulletin for Agency Good Guidance Practices, 72 Fed. Reg. 3432, 3439 (Jan. 25, 2007).

[69] Lincoln v. Vigil, 508 U.S. 182, 197 (1993) (quoting TOM C. CLARK, ATTORNEY GENERAL, ATTORNEY GENERAL'S MANUAL ON THE ADMINISTRATIVE PROCEDURE ACT 30 n.3 (1947)).

[70] It is worth noting that under the traditional form of agency delay—that is, where an agency fails to take a discrete action by a statutory deadline—no rulemaking is required. Often, the agency has not been able to accomplish the required action within the time provided by Congress. In this type of situation, the agency simply has not taken any action; therefore, no rulemaking procedures are required. However, as mentioned above, an agency may be subject to a suit by a party seeking to compel the agency to take action. See 5 U.S.C. § 706.

[71] For example, see Fish and Wildlife Service, Director's Order No. 210 § 2(b) (Feb. 25, 2014), as amended (May 15, 2014) (declaring that, as a matter of enforcement discretion, the Fish and Wildlife Service intends not to enforce the moratorium on the importation of African elephant ivory if the ivory is part of a household move or an inheritance), available at http://www.fws.gov/policy/do210.pdf.

[72] See Heckler, 470 U.S. 821.

[73] See, e.g., Id.

[74] Lincoln, 508 U.S. at 197 (quoting TOM C. CLARK, ATTORNEY GENERAL, ATTORNEY GENERAL'S MANUAL ON THE ADMINISTRATIVE PROCEDURE ACT, at 30 n.3 (1947)).

[75] See General Motors Corp., 742 F.2d at 1565; American Mining Congress, 995 F.2d at 1112.

[76] Internal Revenue Service, Notice 2013-45, NOT-129718-13 (July 3, 2013), available at http://www.irs.gov/pub/irsdrop/n-13-45.PDF.

[77] Id.

[78] See id.

[79] This report does not opine on the legality of the IRS policy, but rather notes that a court would likely find that to release such a statement would not require notice and comment procedures.

[80] Department of the Treasury, Internal Revenue Service, Shared Responsibility for Employers Regarding Health Coverage; Final Rule, 79 Fed. Reg. 8544 (Feb. 12, 2014), available at http://www.gpo.gov/fdsys/pkg/FR-2014-02- 12/pdf/2014-03082.pdf.

[81] Id. at 8574.

[82] Id.

[83] See Community Nutrition Institute, 818 F.2d at 946 n. 4.

[84] It is worth noting that if an agency promulgates a rule after the statutory deadline for issuing such a rule has passed, the delayed rule would still be valid, unless the underlying statute provides otherwise. Barnhart v. Peabody Coal Co., 537 U.S. 149, 155, 171-72 (2003).

In: Delay and Discretion …
Editor: Cory Derricks

ISBN: 978-1-63463-482-3

Chapter 2

ADMINISTRATIVE AGENCIES AND CLAIMS OF UNREASONABLE DELAY: ANALYSIS OF COURT TREATMENT*

Daniel T. Shedd

SUMMARY

One common concern about federal agencies is the speed with which they are able to issue and implement regulations. Federal regulatory schemes can be quite complex, and establishing rules and completing adjudications can sometimes require substantial agency resources and significant amounts of time. However, critics point out that sometimes an agency can simply take too long to a complete task. Commentators and courts have noted that such agency delay can impact the effectiveness of a regulatory scheme. It can also impact regulated entities that must wait for final agency action. In some circumstances, a court may have to determine whether an agency has violated the law by unreasonable delay in taking action. Substantial case law has emerged for how courts will treat agency delay in a variety of circumstances.

* This is an edited, reformatted and augmented version of a Congressional Research Service publication R43013, prepared for Members and Committees of Congress dated March 21, 2013.

Under the Administrative Procedure Act (APA), agency actions must be completed "within a reasonable time." Courts have jurisdiction under the APA to hear claims brought against an agency for unreasonable delay, and the APA provides that courts shall compel any action unreasonably delayed or unlawfully withheld.

When an agency has delayed, but does not have to act by any statutorily imposed deadline, courts are more deferential to the agency's priorities and are less willing to compel an agency to take action. However, if a delay becomes egregious, courts will compel an agency to take prompt action. Generally, courts follow the *TRAC* factors, from *Telecommunications Research & Action Center v. FCC*, to determine whether a delay is unreasonable. The court will see if Congress has established any indication for how quickly the agency should proceed; determine whether a danger to human health is implicated by the delay; consider the agency's competing priorities; evaluate the interests prejudiced by the delay; and determine whether the agency has treated the complaining party disparately from others. A court balances these *TRAC* factors to reach a conclusion on a case-by-case basis. It can be difficult to predict which way a court will decide any particular case. There is no strict rule on how long is too long to wait for an agency action. Therefore, it is important to look at previous cases to see what kinds of delays are determined to be unreasonable.

In addition to the APA's general requirement to act within a reasonable time, Congress may also establish specific deadlines for agency actions by statute. When an agency fails to meet a statutory deadline, courts generally compel the agency to take prompt action. Some courts have determined that a court has no choice but to compel agency action in the face of a missed statutory deadline. For these courts, no balancing is permitted when a deadline has been violated. However, other courts note that a statutory deadline is merely one of the factors to consider when determining whether the delay is unreasonable. For these courts, the *TRAC* factors are still evaluated to determine whether the court should compel the agency to act after a deadline has been missed.

Judicial remedies for delayed agency actions are somewhat limited. The Supreme Court has ruled that a court is permitted to compel an agency to take action, but cannot determine what conclusion the agency shall ultimately reach on the issue. Furthermore, the Supreme Court has also established that agency rules still maintain the force of law, even when they are promulgated after a statutory deadline. Therefore, a court's only remedy for unreasonable agency delay is essentially to impose a deadline on the agency.

Introduction

Congress maintains an active interest in the effective implementation of regulatory systems adopted by federal agencies. A common concern is the pace at which agencies establish rules and complete adjudications. Commentators and courts have noted that agency delay can impact the effectiveness of a regulatory system.[1] Delays can also negatively affect regulated entities that must wait for final agency action. As one court noted: "Quite simply, excessive delay saps the public confidence in an agency's ability to discharge its responsibilities and creates uncertainty for the parties, who must incorporate the potential effect of possible agency decisionmaking into future plans."[2] Substantial case law has emerged on how courts will treat agency delay in a variety of circumstances.

The Administrative Procedure Act (APA) imposes a general time restraint on administrative agencies—they must act within a "reasonable time."[3] If a person meets the necessary standing requirements, he can sue the agency for failing to act within a reasonable time. However, when there is no hard deadline imposed on the agency, courts are often reluctant to compel an agency to act and often allow an agency to set its own priorities.

In addition to the general timing requirements imposed by the APA, Congress also has the power to require agencies to act on issues within a specific time frame by establishing a statutory deadline in the agency's enabling statute. When an agency fails to meet a statutory deadline, courts are more willing to compel the agency to take prompt action.

Judicial remedies available for delayed agency actions are somewhat limited. Generally, a court is restricted to ordering an agency to act by a specific deadline. The following sections outline the timing requirements imposed by the APA, discuss the available judicial remedies when actions are found to be unreasonably delayed, and provide an examination of cases where courts have been asked to compel agency action. Finally, the report concludes with a discussion of legislative tools that Congress can use to try to set agency priorities.

Administrative Procedure Act (APA)

The APA does not provide any concrete time limits for agency actions. Instead, the APA leaves most deadlines to be established in the particular agency's enabling statute, if at all. However, the APA states that "within a reasonable time, each agency shall proceed to conclude a matter presented to it."[4] Further, the APA states that courts shall "compel agency action unlawfully withheld or unreasonably delayed."[5] As such, the APA provides individuals with a cause of action when agency action has been unreasonably delayed.

A court may hear a claim for unreasonable delay despite the fact that the agency has yet to take a final action on the subject. Generally, under Section 704 of the APA, a court does not have jurisdiction over an agency matter until the agency action is final.[6] However, a court can have jurisdiction over a matter pending before an agency when a party claims that there has been an unlawful or unreasonable delay. In *Norton v. SUWA*, the Supreme Court stated that "when an agency is compelled by law to act within a certain time period ... a court can compel the agency to act."[7] The United States Court of Appeals for the District of Columbia Circuit (D.C. Circuit) has also noted that the language of the APA indicates that Congress intended the courts to play a role in ensuring that agencies fulfill their obligation to act within a reasonable time,[8] and other circuits have noted that a claim of unreasonable delay qualifies for judicial review despite a lack of "final agency action."[9]

Claims for unreasonable delay can be brought under the APA against an agency in court. However, a claim of unreasonable delay can only be brought against an agency for actions that the agency is legally obligated to take. The Supreme Court has stated that "a claim under § 706(1) [of the APA] can proceed only when a plaintiff asserts that an agency failed to take a *discrete* agency action that it is *required* to take."[10] If taking a certain action is "committed to agency discretion by law," then no claim can be made against the agency for failing to take such an action.[11] In other words, an agency must be required to act by law in order to establish a claim that the agency has unreasonably delayed in acting.

REMEDIES FOR UNREASONABLY DELAYED ACTIONS

Before discussing how a court determines whether an unreasonable delay has occurred, it is important to understand the limitations on available judicial remedies. When a court determines that an action has been unreasonably delayed, it must then decide what remedy to provide the plaintiff. First, although a court can order an agency to take prompt action on an issue, the Supreme Court has declared that a court cannot dictate what conclusion the agency should reach.[12] The Court stated that when an agency misses a deadline, a court can issue "a judicial decree under the APA requiring the prompt issuance of regulations, but not a judicial decree setting forth the content of those regulations."[13] For example, if an agency must determine critical habitat for an endangered species, the court can direct the agency to act immediately, but the court cannot determine which habitat is critical. Furthermore, the Supreme Court has stated that regulations issued after a deadline has passed still maintain the force of law, despite the tardiness of their promulgation.[14] Therefore, a plaintiff cannot challenge the validity of regulations merely based on their promulgation after a deadline. Thus, judicial remedies are generally limited to imposing deadlines on the agency.

Courts take varying approaches when fashioning a remedy for an agency action that has been unduly delayed. In some cases a court will order an agency to act promptly.[15] In other situations, a court might impose a deadline on the agency.[16] Sometimes courts merely direct the agency to impose a deadline on itself, which the court will accept unless the agency's proposed deadline is unreasonable.[17] Additionally, courts will often maintain jurisdiction over the case until the agency action has been completed.[18] In these situations, the court will require the agency to file regular reports with the court detailing the progress the agency has made on the action to ensure the agency is actively working to comply.[19] Examples of how courts fashion remedies are provided in the cases discussed in this report.

COMPELLING ACTIONS UNREASONABLY DELAYED WITH NO STATUTORY DEADLINES

Generally, courts tend to avoid compelling agency action because they do not want to impose agendas on the more politically accountable regulatory agencies. Courts will look to enabling statutes to see if there are statutory time requirements imposed on the agency. When there is no statutory deadline for the agency action, courts tend to be more deferential to the agency's priorities. According to the *Blackletter Statement of Federal Administrative Law* from the American Bar Association:

> An agency's delay in completing a pending action as to which there is no statutory deadline may not be held unlawful unless the delay is unreasonable in light of such considerations as the agency's need to set priorities among lawful objectives, the challenger's interest in prompt

action, and any relevant indications of legislative intent. In considering such challenges courts are deferential to agencies' allocation of their own limited resources.[20]

The D.C. Circuit, in *Telecommunications Research & Action Center v. FCC* ("*TRAC*"),[21] established guidelines to consider when determining whether an agency delay warrants mandamus[22] compelling the agency to act. The court stated that "[i]n the context of a claim of unreasonable delay, the first stage of judicial inquiry is to consider whether the agency's delay is so egregious as to warrant mandamus."[23] The court then enumerated several factors, known as the *TRAC* factors, to consider when answering this question:

> (1) the time agencies take to make decisions must be governed by a "rule of reason;" (2) where Congress has provided a timetable or other indication of the speed with which it expects the agency to proceed in the enabling statute, that statutory scheme may supply content for this rule of reason; (3) delays that might be reasonable in the sphere of economic regulation are less tolerable when human health and welfare are at stake; (4) the court should consider the effect of expediting delayed action on agency activities of a higher or competing priority; (5) the court should also take into account the nature and extent of the interests prejudiced by delay; and (6) the court need not find any impropriety lurking behind agency lassitude in order to hold that agency action is unreasonably delayed.[24]

Although the *TRAC* factors are widely cited with regard to whether a court should issue mandamus to compel agency action, courts have also been quick to point out that "mandamus is a drastic remedy, suitable only in extraordinary situations."[25]

Delay in Adjudication Proceedings with No Statutory Deadline

In cases where there are no statutory deadlines imposed, agency delay of several years on an adjudication may pass before a court issues a writ of mandamus. Decisions seem to vary, and it can be difficult to predict how a court will rule on a question of unreasonable delay. The D.C. Circuit has noted that "[t]here is no per se rule as to how long is too long to wait for agency action,"[26] and it can be hard to determine which *TRAC* factor a court will decide to rely on most heavily. As a result, it appears that each claim of agency delay is determined on a case-by-case basis. This section explores some court decisions to illustrate the difficulty in determining which way a court will rule on a claim of unreasonable delay. For example, in one circumstance, a court determined a delay of 10 years on reaching a decision to be reasonable,[27] while in another situation, a court determined an eight-year delay to be unreasonable.[28]

In *TRAC*, the petitioners claimed that the Federal Communications Commission (FCC) had unreasonably delayed in determining whether AT&T should reimburse ratepayers for certain alleged overcharges.[29] Despite the fact that the proceeding had taken five years and had not yet been resolved, the court decided that the delay did not warrant mandamus in light of the fact that mere economic interests were involved and that the agency had assured the court that it was working expeditiously to resolve the proceeding.[30] Instead of compelling the agency to act, the court required the FCC to provide the anticipated date of resolution and maintained jurisdiction in order to ensure that the agency proceeded accordingly.[31]

In *Potomac Elec. Power Co. v. ICC*,[32] a court found an eight-year adjudication to determine the justness and reasonableness of a railroad's rates to be unreasonable.[33] In this case, the court issued a writ of mandamus and required a final agency order to be issued within sixty days.[34] In justifying the writ of mandamus, despite the fact that the matter merely involved economic interests, the court pointed to legislative history that indicated that Congress wanted the Interstate Commerce Commission (ICC) to act quickly in these rate proceedings.[35] However, in *Kokajko v. FERC*,[36] despite the presence of similar legislative history—"FERC is statutorily required to give preference and speedy consideration to questions concerning increased rates or charges for the transmission or sale of electric energy"—the court determined that five years was not an unreasonable amount of time to wait for a final agency determination[37] and dismissed the petitioner's claim.[38] In *Kokajko*, the court focused on the fact that the case merely involved an economic interest and that there was no "significant length of unexplained agency inaction."[39] The court stated, however, that "a five year delay is approaching the threshold of unreasonableness."[40]

The United States Court of Appeals for the Fourth Circuit, in *In re City of Virginia Beach*,[41] determined that mandamus was not warranted for a four and one-half year wait for approval of a water pipeline construction project.[42] Although the court noted that the water pipeline affected "human health and welfare," the court declined to compel immediate agency action in light of the Federal Energy Regulatory Commission's (FERC) assurances that the project was a high priority and would be expedited.[43] Because the delay was not entirely caused by FERC, the court determined that mandamus was not warranted despite the fact that the court was "[not] happy about the overall time elapsed."[44]

The United States Court of Appeals for the Eighth Circuit upheld a ten-year delay by the Citizenship and Immigration Services (CIS) on an application for permanent residence.[45] The court noted that the application was given considerable attention by the agency and that the delays were partially caused by changes in legislation regarding required investigations of applicants.[46] The court held that the agency had thus not unreasonably delayed in reaching a final determination on the proceeding within 10 years.[47]

Delay in Rulemaking Proceedings with No Statutory Deadline

Courts have treated an agency's delay in promulgating rules similarly to agency delay in adjudication procedures. Courts still apply the *TRAC* factors when determining whether a delay is unreasonable in the rulemaking setting. Again, it can be difficult to predict whether a court will compel an agency to act on a claim for unreasonable delay when there is no statutory deadline.

In one case involving rulemaking proceedings, the court found that a three-year delay by the Environmental Protection Agency (EPA) was reasonable.[48] The EPA had undertaken a rulemaking to determine if it should regulate strip mines under the Clean Air Act. The court noted that "absent a precise statutory timetable or other factors counseling expeditious action, an agency's control over the timetable of a rulemaking procedure is entitled to considerable deference."[49] The court again applied the *TRAC* factors and considered the fact that human health and welfare was at stake. It also noted that the agency had been progressing on the rule by holding public meetings, accepting comments, and issuing reports on the issue. After weighing all the considerations, the court stated "given the complexity of the issues facing EPA and the highly controversial nature of the proposal, agency deliberation for less than three years ... can hardly be considered unreasonable."[50]

However, in a different case, *Public Citizen Health Research Group v. Auchter*,[51] the same court held that the Occupational Safety and Health Administration's (OSHA) three-year delay in promulgating a final rule for ethylene oxide (EtO) safety standards was unreasonably delayed. Although this case was decided prior to *TRAC*, the court still made reference to the same factors. It stated that "[d]elays that might be altogether reasonable in the sphere of economic regulation are less tolerable when human lives are at stake."[52] Emphasizing the delay's potential impact to human health,[53] the court ordered that a notice of proposed rulemaking be issued within thirty days and stated that it expected a final rule within a year.[54]

In *In re International Chemical Workers Union*,[55] the court determined that a six-year delay in promulgating a rule regarding cadmium exposure safety standards was unreasonable. In this case the agency acknowledged that a new standard for cadmium exposure limits was necessary, but repeatedly pushed back the expected release date for the final rule. The court used the *TRAC* standards and noted that the purpose of the OSHA statute was to protect the health of American workers. It balanced this against the agency's limited resources and other competing activities. In the end, the court accepted the agency's "estimate of the additional time it needs to complete the final stages of the rulemaking," but warned that any additional postponement "would violate [the] court's order." [56] The agency was forced to promulgate a final standard within seven months of the court order.

These few examples show that it can be challenging to pinpoint when a court will compel agency action in both rulemaking and adjudication proceedings when there are no statutory deadlines in place.

Compelling Delayed Actions That Violate Statutory Deadlines

Courts more readily compel agencies to act in cases where there is a statutory deadline imposed on an agency.[57] The Supreme Court declared, in *Norton v. SUWA*, that "when an agency is compelled by law to act within a certain time period ... a court can compel the agency to act."[58] Some lower courts have made a distinction between actions "unlawfully withheld" (actions that are delayed beyond a statutory deadline) and actions "unreasonably delayed" (actions that are only governed by the APA's "reasonable time" provision) and have determined that a missed statutory deadline compels the court to mandate prompt agency action. Although it is commonplace for courts to compel agencies to act if a deadline has been missed, some courts, as illustrated below, may decline to compel an agency to act in such circumstances. For example, despite the existence of a statutory deadline, the D.C. Circuit still applies the *TRAC* test to determine whether it is appropriate to issue an order compelling the agency to act.

In *Forrest Guardians v. Babbitt*,[59] the United States Court of Appeals for the Tenth Circuit (Tenth Circuit) stated that when an agency fails to act by a "statutorily imposed absolute deadline," the action has been "unlawfully withheld" and the court has no choice but to compel the agency to act.[60] The Tenth Circuit noted that Section 706(1) of the APA states that courts "shall compel agency action unlawfully withheld," and declared that the court, because of Congress's use of the word "shall," had no discretion on the issue.[61] The court stated that although the *TRAC* factors might be helpful when considering action guided by a mere general timing provision, the court could not apply the *TRAC* test to situations where an agency has failed to meet a specific statutory deadline.[62] The court remanded the case and directed the district court to order the Secretary to "issue a final critical habitat designation ... as soon as possible, without regard to the Secretary's other priorities under the [Endangered Species Act]."[63]

Similarly, the United States Court of Appeals for the Ninth Circuit (Ninth Circuit) has held that a court must compel agency action when the agency fails to comply with a statutory deadline. In *Biodiversity Legal Foundation v. Badgley*,[64] the Ninth Circuit found that it was required to issue an injunction to require the Fish and Wildlife Service (FWS) to comply with a twelve-month deadline imposed by the Endangered Species Act.[65] Although the Ninth Circuit acknowledged that it follows the *TRAC* standard in cases involving general timing provisions, the court stated that "Congress has specifically provided a deadline for performance by the Service, so no balancing of factors is required or permitted."[66] The court stated that the missed deadline "compelled the court to grant injunctive relief" and that the "court had no discretion to consider the Service's stated priorities."[67]

Other courts, however, do not follow this distinction. For these courts, a statutory deadline acts only as one of the *factors* to consider when applying the *TRAC* test for unreasonable delay and is not, by itself, determinative. Although a deadline will weigh heavily in favor of compelling an agency to act, some courts have declined to order an agency to take action even in the face of deadlines that have long passed.[68]

The United States District Court for the District of Columbia, in *Ctr. for Biological Diversity v. Pirie*,[69] criticized the reasoning followed by the Tenth Circuit in the *Forrest Guardians* decision. Although the court acknowledged that Section 706 of the APA states that the courts "*shall* compel agency action unlawfully withheld or unreasonably delayed,"[70] the court determined that courts still have discretion when determining whether to issue a writ of mandamus or injunction against an agency.[71] The court pointed to Section 702 of the APA,[72] and declared that the language of this section preserved the courts' equitable discretion in these cases: "Because 702 of the APA explicitly states that a court retains equitable discretion, this Court cannot hold that Congress has clearly and unequivocally limited that discretion under the APA."[73] Therefore, the court determined that it is not forced to compel agency action, even if the agency has missed a statutory deadline.

In its opinion from *In Re Barr Laboratories, Inc.*,[74] the D.C. Circuit noted that "a finding that delay is unreasonable does not, alone, justify judicial intervention."[75] In this case, the Food and Drug Administration (FDA) had missed a statutory deadline for reviewing "generic drug" applications.[76] By statute, the FDA was supposed to review these applications within 180 days.[77] However, the FDA estimated that its response time could range from 389 to 669 days.[78] Barr Laboratories sought mandamus compelling the agency to review its application and claimed that, by missing the statutory deadline, the FDA had unreasonably delayed.[79] The court responded: "Though we agree with Barr that FDA's sluggish pace violates a statutory deadline, we conclude that this is not an appropriate case for equitable relief."[80] The court looked at all of the *TRAC* factors and determined that mandamus was not appropriate despite the fact that the FDA failed to meet their statutory deadline by a significant margin.[81] The court noted that simply putting one drug manufacturer's case to the front of the line would necessarily push other similar cases further back and would not ultimately promote Congress's objective of having all applications dealt with swiftly.[82] The court did not want to determine the agency's priorities;[83] however, the court did note that if Barr Laboratories had been singled out for mistreatment, an order of mandamus might have been appropriate.[84]

Finally, the D.C. Circuit held that a nine-year delay by the United States Coast Guard, in the face of a one-year deadline for promulgating regulations regarding oil tanker standards, was unreasonable.[85] The court ordered the agency to take "prompt" action.[86] However, it applied the *TRAC* factors, indicating that merely missing the deadline was not, by itself, enough for the court to issue mandamus to compel the agency to act.[87]

The *TRAC* factors remain the most common approach to determining whether agency actions have been unreasonably delayed in both rulemaking proceedings and adjudicatory proceedings. One potential problem with the *TRAC* test is that it fails to provide any clear answer to whether an agency has delayed unreasonably.[88] Even the D.C. Circuit acknowledges "[t]here is no per se rule as to how long is too long to wait for agency action"[89] and that the *TRAC* balancing test "sometimes suffers from vagueness."[90] With no clear standard, it can be difficult for regulated entities to estimate when they could expect agency action finally to occur or when it would be appropriate to sue an agency for their delays. However, it seems that two factors always tend to receive ample discussion from the courts. First, statutory deadlines appear to be a significant factor in determining a case of unreasonable delay. When Congress signifies that it wants an agency to prioritize an action, the courts are more willing to enforce that priority. Second, courts appear to be more willing to compel an agency to act when the action involves public health or safety, compared to mere economic interests. Ultimately, however, the determination is made on a fact specific, case-by-case basis.

LEGISLATIVE TOOLS TO COMPEL AGENCY ACTION

Congress often attempts to press agencies to resolve issues and promulgate rules in swift fashion. Perhaps Congress's most effective tool, discussed above, is the statutory deadline. Although in some circumstances courts will decline to enforce the deadline on the agency, claims for unreasonable delay are vastly more successful when there is a statutory deadline imposed by Congress.[91] Recent scholarship also notes that rulemakings that are undertaken with an imposed statutory deadline are, on average, completed sooner than similar rules with no deadline imposed.[92] It is important to note, however, that when overly imposing deadlines are placed on agency action, agencies often have to act hastily and may reduce the time available for public participation in a rulemaking.[93] In some circumstances, a tight deadline can lead an agency to avoid normal notice and comment procedures by invoking the "good cause" provision under the APA.[94]

Another tool available to Congress is the imposition of "hammer" provisions.[95] These provisions, which may be written in tandem with a statutory deadline, dictate what is to happen if a regulatory deadline is missed. These provisions, therefore, impose a consequence if the agency fails to meet the statutory deadline. The consequences for missing a deadline vary. Some laws establish a regulatory scheme that will be put in place if a deadline is missed;[96] others mandate that the agency's *proposed* rule would go into effect if a final rule is not promulgated by the deadline.[97] At least one law has withheld funding from an agency until certain rules are promulgated.[98] Although these provisions can force an agency to act quickly, they can also be difficult for Congress to establish. For example, for laws that require a congressionally mandated regulatory scheme to go into effect if the agency misses a deadline, subject matter expertise may be helpful or necessary to establish a statutorily imposed regulatory scheme.

Congress also maintains the "power of the purse" and can place restrictions on appropriations or threaten to do so if Congress determines that an agency is failing to act in a timely manner. Finally, in the event that an agency is taking too long to take an action, Congress also has the ability to exert political pressure on the agency. Congressional committees can call oversight hearings to question an agency leader regarding delays.[99] Individual members are also permitted to express their concerns to agencies and often send letters to pressure agencies to act promptly on certain issues.[100] Although courts will ultimately determine whether an action has been delayed unreasonably, Congress is able to use these tools to try to establish priorities for the federal agencies' agendas.

End Notes

[1] See, e.g., Michael D. Sant'Ambrogio, Agency Delays: How a Principal-Agent Approach Can Inform Judicial and Executive Branch Review of Agency Foot-Dragging, 79 Geo. Wash. L. Rev. 1381; Potomac Electric Power Co. v. ICC, 702 F.2d 1026, 1034 (D.C. Cir. 1983).

[2] Potomac Electric Power Co. v. ICC, 702 F.2d 1026, 1034 (D.C. Cir. 1983).

[3] 5 U.S.C. §555(b).

[4] 5 U.S.C. §555(b).

[5] Id. at §706(1).

[6] Id. at §704 ("[F]inal agency action for which there is no other adequate remedy in a court [is] subject to judicial review.").

[7] Norton v. S. Utah Wilderness Alliance, 542 U.S. 55, 65 (2004).

[8] Telecommunications Research & Action Center v. FCC, 750 F.2d 70, 77–78 (D.C. Cir. 1984) ("TRAC") ("[S]ection 706(1) coupled with section 555(b) does indicate a congressional view that agencies should act within reasonable time frames and that courts designated by statute to review agency actions may play an important role in compelling agency action that has been improperly withheld or unreasonably delayed."). Section 555(b) states that agencies should conclude matters "within a reasonable time," and Section 706(1) states that courts "shall ... compel agency action unlawfully withheld or unreasonably delayed." 5 U.S.C. §§555(b), 706(1).

[9] See, e.g. Gordon v. Norton, 322 F.3d 1213, 1220 (10th Cir. 2003) ("An agency's failure to act ... can become a final agency action in three situations: 1) if the agency "affirmatively rejects a proposed course of action; 2) if the agency delays unreasonably in responding to a request for action; and 3) if the agency delays in responding until the requested action would be ineffective.").

[10] Norton v. SUWA, 542 U.S. at 64 (emphasis in original).

[11] 5 U.S.C. §701(a)(1), (2).

[12] Norton v. SUWA, 542 U.S. at 65.

[13] Id.

[14] Barnhart v. Peabody Coal Co., 537 U.S. 149, 155, 171-72 (2003).

[15] See, e.g., Forrest Guardians v. Babbitt, 174 F.3d 1178, 1193 (10th Cir. 1998) (ordering agency to issue a final rule "as soon as possible").

[16] See, e.g., Public Citizen Health Research Group v. Auchter, 702 F.2d 1150, 1158–59 (DC. Cir. 1983) (ordering agency to promulgate a notice of proposed rulemaking within 30 days).

[17] See, e.g., In re International Chemical Workers Union, 958 F.2d 1144, 1150 (D.C. Cir. 1992) (holding that the agency's estimated need for additional time is reasonable, but any additional postponement would be a violation of the court's order).

[18] See, e.g., In re United Mine Workers of America International Union, 190 F.3d 545, 546 (DC Cir. 1999).

[19] Id.

[20] Section of Administrative Law & Regulatory Practice, American Bar Ass'n, A Blackletter Statement of Federal Administrative Law, 54 Admin L. Rev. 1, 44 (2002).

[21] 750 F.2d 70 (D.C. Cir. 1984) ("TRAC").

[22] Mandamus is an order from a court directing a party to take a certain action, such as commence a rulemaking or complete an adjudication.

[23] Id. at 79.

[24] Id. at 80 (internal quotations omitted).

[25] Wellesley v. FERC, 829 F.2d 275, 277 (1st Cir. 1987); see also, e.g., Kerr v. United States District Court, 426 U.S. 394, 402 (1976).

[26] In re Barr Laboratories, Inc., 930 F.2d 72, 76 (D.C. Cir. 1991).

[27] Debba v. Heinauer, 366 Fed. Appx. 696 (8th Cir. 2010). This case is discussed below.

[28] Potomac Electric Power Co. v. ICC, 702 F.2d 1026 (D.C. Cir. 1983). This case is discussed below.

[29] TRAC, 750 F.2d at 72.

[30] Id. at 80–81.

[31] Id. at 81.

[32] 702 F.2d 1026 (D.C. Cir. 1983).

[33] Id. at 1027–28.

[34] Id. at 1035.

[35] Id. at 1033–34.

[36] 837 F.2d 524 (1st Cir. 1988).

[37] Id. at 526.

[38] Id.

[39] Id.

[40] Id.; see also Wellesley v. FERC, 829 F.2d 275 (1st Cir. 1987) (holding that a 14 month delay on a rate proceeding did not warrant mandamus, despite legislative history suggesting that FERC should act quickly, and stating "the cases in which courts have afforded relief have involved delays of years" not months).

[41] 42 F.3d 881 (4th Cir. 1994).

[42] Id.

[43] Id. at 886.

[44] Id.

[45] Debba v. Heinauer, 366 Fed. Appx. 696 (8th Cir. 2010).

[46] Id. at 699.

[47] Id.

[48] Sierra Club v. Thomas, 828 F.2d 783 (D.C. Cir. 1987).

[49] Id. at 797.

[50] Id. at 799.

[51] 702 F.2d 1150 (D.C. Cir. 1983).

[52] Id. at 1157.

[53] Id. ("Three years from announced intent to regulate to final rule is simply too long given the significant risk of grave danger EtO poses to the lives of current workers and the lives and well-being of their offspring.").

[54] Id. at 1158–59.

[55] 958 F.2d 1144 (D.C. Cir. 1992).

[56] Id. at 1150.

[57] Michael D. Sant'Ambrogio, Agency Delays: How a Principal-Agent Approach Can Inform Judicial and Executive Branch Review of Agency Foot-Dragging, 79 Geo. Wash. L. Rev. 1381, 1414 (2011) ("Courts will generally compel agency action that violates a clear statutory deadline."); Eric Biber, The Importance of Resource Allocation in Administrative Law, 60 Admin. L. Rev. 1, 39 (2008) (noting that claims become significantly easier to win when there is a statutory deadline involved).

[58] Norton v. SUWA, 542 U.S. at 65.

[59] 174 F.3d 1178 (10th Cir. 1998). This case involved the U.S. Fish and Wildlife Service's failure to make a final determination on petitions to list certain species as endangered or threatened under the Endangered Species Act by the statutorily imposed twelve-month deadline. Id.

[60] Id. at 1190.

[61] Id. at 1187–93. However, the Tenth Circuit noted that when an agency is only guided by a "general timing provision," such as a requirement to act "within a reasonable time," the court does have discretion to decide whether the delay has been unreasonable. Id. at 1190–91.

[62] Id. at 1191.

[63] Id. at 1193.

[64] 309 F.3d 1166 (9th Cir. 2002).

[65] Id. at 1178.

[66] Id.

[67] Id. at 1178.

[68] See In re Barr Laboratories, Inc., 930 F.3d 72, 74 (D.C. Cir. 1991) ("The issue before us, then, is not whether the FDA's sluggishness has violated a statutory mandate—it has—but whether we should exercise our equitable powers to enforce the deadline."). This case is discussed below.

[69] 201 F. Supp. 2d 113 (D.D.C. 2002). Although this case did not involve an agency delay, it does show that the court found that Section 706 does not require a court to issue a writ of mandamus or an injunction when an agency is in violation of a statute.

[70] Id. at 118.

[71] Id. at 119 (Citing Sanchez-Espinoza v. Reagan, 770 F.2d 202, 207–08 (D.C. Cir. 1985).

[72] Section 702 of the APA states that "Nothing herein affects other limitations on judicial review or the power or duty of the court to dismiss any action or deny relief on any other appropriate legal or equitable ground." 5 U.S.C. §702 (2006).

[73] Ctr. for Biological Diversity v. Pirie, 201 F. Supp. at 119.

[74] 930 F.2d 72 (D.C. Cir. 1991).

[75] Id. at 75.

[76] Id. at 73–74.

[77] Id. at 74.

[78] Id.

[79] See id. at 73.
[80] Id.
[81] Id. at 74–76.
[82] Id. at 75.
[83] "The agency is in a unique—and authoritative—position to view its projects as a whole, estimate the prospects for each, and allocate its resources in the optimal way. Such budget flexibility as Congress has allowed the agency is not for us to hijack.... While Congress clearly intended a faster track for generic drug applications in general, it did not choose a super-priority for Barr, and it did not address the trade-off between strict compliance with the 180-day deadline and the FDA's disposition of its other projects with enough clarity to guide judicial intervention." Id.
[84] Id. at 75-76; but see Sandoz, Inc. v. Leavitt, 427 F. Supp. 2d 29 (D.D.C. 2006) (applying the TRAC factors and holding that a 1000 day response time by the FDA on a similar generic drug application was unreasonable in light of the fact that the FDA seemed to treat the plaintiff disparately from other generic drug applicants).
[85] In re Blue Water Network and Ocean Advocates, 234 F.3d 1305 (D.C. Cir. 2000).
[86] Id. at 1316.
[87] Id. at 1315–16.
[88] Professor Sant'Ambrogio notes that "[d]ue to the lack of clarity in the doctrine, courts can use the TRAC analysis to support virtually any conclusion they want to reach." Michael D. Sant'Ambrogio, Agency Delays: How a Principal-Agent Approach Can Inform Judicial and Executive Branch Review of Agency Foot-Dragging, 79 Geo. Wash. L. Rev. 1381, 1443 (2011).
[89] In re Am. Rivers & Idaho Rivers United, 372 F.3d 413, 419 (D.C. Cir. 2004).
[90] TRAC, 750 F.2d at 80.
[91] See Michael D. Sant'Ambrogio, Agency Delays: How a Principal-Agent Approach Can Inform Judicial and Executive Branch Review of Agency Foot-Dragging, 79 Geo. Wash. L. Rev. 1381, 1414 ("Courts will generally compel agency action that violates a clear statutory deadline."); Eric Biber, The Importance of Resource Allocation in Administrative Law, 60 Admin. L. Rev. 1, 39 (2008) (noting that claims become significantly easier to win when there is a statutory deadline involved).
[92] Jacob E. Gerson & Anne Joseph O'Connell, Deadlines in Administrative Law, 156 U. Pa. L. Rev. 923, 945–950 (2008).
[93] Id. at 945.
[94] Id. at 956–59; 5 U.S.C. §553(b)(3)(B) (an agency may avoid notice and comment procedures "when the agency for good cause finds ... that notice and public procedure thereon are impracticable").
[95] See Jeffrey S. Lubbers, A Guide to Federal Agency Rulemaking 15–16 (4th ed. 2006).
[96] See, e.g., 42 U.S.C. §6924(d)(1-2).
[97] See, e.g., The Nutrition Labeling and Education Act of 1990, P.L. 101-535.
[98] See Department of Transportation and Related Agencies Appropriations Act, 1988, P.L. 100-202, Title 1.
[99] See Jeffrey S. Lubbers, A Guide to Federal Agency Rulemaking 18–19.
[100] See id.; see also, e.g., Letter from various members of Congress to Dr. Margaret A. Hamburg, Commissioner of Food and Drugs, U.S. Food and Drug Administration (May 6, 2011) available at http://schakowsky.house.gov/images/ stories/Letter_to_FDA_on_Dangerous_ Chemicals_in_Brazilian_Blowout_Hair_Treatments.pdf.

In: Delay and Discretion …
Editor: Cory Derricks
ISBN: 978-1-63463-482-3

Chapter 3

THE TAKE CARE CLAUSE AND EXECUTIVE DISCRETION IN THE ENFORCEMENT OF LAW*

Todd Garvey

SUMMARY

The Take Care Clause would appear to stand for two, at times diametrically opposed propositions—one imposing a "duty" upon the President and the other viewing the Clause as a source of Presidential "power." Primarily, the Take Care Clause has been interpreted as placing an obligation on both the President and those under his supervision to comply with and execute clear statutory directives as enacted by Congress. However, the Supreme Court has also construed the Clause as ensuring Presidential control over the enforcement of federal law. As a result, courts generally will not review Presidential enforcement decisions, including the decision of whether to initiate a criminal prosecution or administrative enforcement action in response to a violation of federal law.

In situations where an agency refrains from bringing an enforcement action, courts have historically been cautious in reviewing the agency determination—generally holding that these nonenforcement decisions

* This is an edited, reformatted and augmented version of a Congressional Research Service publication R43708, prepared for Members and Committees of Congress dated September 4, 2014.

are "committed to agency discretion" and therefore not subject to judicial review under the Administrative Procedure Act. The seminal case on this topic is Heckler v. Chaney, in which the Supreme Court held that an "agency's decision not to take enforcement action should be presumed immune from judicial review."

However, the Court also clearly indicated that the presumption against judicial review of agency nonenforcement decisions may be overcome in a variety of specific situations. For example, a court may review an agency nonenforcement determination "where the substantive statute has provided guidelines for the agency to follow in exercising its enforcement powers," or where the agency has "'consciously and expressly adopted a general policy' that is so extreme as to amount to an abdication of its statutory responsibilities."

As such, it would appear that Congress may overcome the presumption of nonreviewability and restrict executive discretion through statute by expressly providing "meaningful standards" for the manner in which the agency may exercise its enforcement powers.

Nevertheless, legislation that can be characterized as significantly restricting the exercise of executive branch enforcement decisions, in either the criminal, civil, or administrative context, could raise questions under the separation of powers.

The Obama Administration has faced significant scrutiny following a series of determinations in which the relevant federal agency charged with the implementation of a given statute has chosen to limit or delay the enforcement of specific provisions of federal law.[1] These nonenforcement, under enforcement, or delayed enforcement decisions have generally been implemented through stated agency policies directing officials *not* to take action to ensure compliance with statutory requirements that federal law imposes upon a third party. Notably, these policies have been grounded in practical or policy considerations, and have not been based on any argument that the statutory provisions themselves are unconstitutional or otherwise invalid.[2] Instead, the Administration has largely justified its inaction as consistent with a proper exercise of enforcement discretion, a legal doctrine that generally shields executive branch enforcement decisions, including the determination of whether to initiate a criminal, civil, or administrative enforcement action, from judicial review. This report focuses on two distinct forms of enforcement discretion: prosecutorial discretion, exercised in the criminal context; and administrative enforcement discretion, exercised in the administrative context.

The Department of Justice (DOJ) has cited prosecutorial discretion as the basis for its efforts to curtail the enforcement of the federal Controlled Substances Act (CSA) in states that have adopted both medical and recreational marijuana legalization initiatives.[3] Although the possession, cultivation, or distribution of marijuana remains a clear federal crime, the DOJ has directed federal prosecutors to "not focus federal resources [] on individuals whose actions are in clear and unambiguous compliance with existing state laws providing for the medical use of marijuana."[4] Rather, U.S. Attorneys have been directed to prioritize investigative and prosecutorial resources on persons whose actions relate to identified federal priorities such as distribution to minors, the participation of criminal enterprises and cartels, or the use of marijuana on federal property.[5]

In 2012, the Secretary of Homeland Security relied on the doctrine of administrative enforcement discretion in a memorandum setting forth guidelines on how to "enforce the Nation's immigration laws against certain young people who were brought to this country as children and know only this country as home."[6] The directive provided that, rather than use limited agency removal resources on low priority deportation cases, immigration officers should exercise their discretion to forego enforcement actions, for at least a period of time, against a specific class of individuals who unlawfully entered the United States as children, have not committed certain crimes, and meet other key requirements.[7] It has been argued, however, that the Secretary's memorandum contravenes statutory mandates under the Immigration and Nationality Act which, opponents of the policy assert, *require* that aliens who entered the country without inspection be "detained for removal proceedings."[8] In 2013 and 2014, the Administration utilized enforcement discretion to justify delays in the enforcement of a number of provisions of the Affordable care act (ACA), including the law's employer mandate and minimum coverage requirements. These provisions were to take effect beginning on January 1, 2014. In July 2013, the Treasury Department announced that enforcement of the ACA's new excise tax on employers with 50 or more employees that fail to provide affordable health coverage (the "employer mandate") would be delayed for one year, until 2015.[9] In February 2014, the Administration announced that employers with at least 50 but fewer than 100 full-time equivalent employees would have an additional year to comply with the mandate.[10] Similarly, the Centers for Medicare and Medicaid Services announced in November 2013 that it was adopting a "transitional policy," under which health insurers can continue to offer coverage that fails to meet certain statutorily required minimum standards for private health insurance under the ACA without threat of federal enforcement consequences.[11]

In contrast to the Administration position, some Members of Congress have asserted that these unilateral Presidential nonenforcement determinations upset the separation of powers, harm Congress as an institution and a coordinate branch of government, and are in direct violation of the President's constitutional obligation to "take Care that the Laws be faithfully executed..."[12] Although the House has held hearings addressing the issue and has approved legislation that would require the Administration to provide Congress with a report describing the legal grounds for any nonenforcement decisions, the Senate has not concurred with the House's objections.[13]

As a result, the House appears to be focusing on the judicial process as a means of addressing the Administration's nonenforcement policies. The ENFORCE the Law Act of 2014, which passed the House in March 2014, would establish an expedited process by which either house of Congress could file a lawsuit challenging a "formal or informal policy, practice, or procedure to refrain from enforcing, applying, following, or administering any provision of a Federal statute, rule, regulation, program, policy, or other law in violation of the requirement that the President take care that the laws be faithfully executed..."[14] In addition, the House approved a joint resolution that would authorize the Speaker—through the House General Counsel—to file a lawsuit seeking "any appropriate relief regarding the failure of the President, the head of any department or agency, or any other officer or employee of the executive branch, to act in a manner consistent with that official's duties under the Constitution and laws of the United States with respect to implementation of any provision of the [ACA]."[15] In light of these ongoing controversies, this report will address the President's general obligation to "take Care that the Laws be faithfully executed." The report will then discuss the limited role the judicial branch has traditionally adopted in reviewing discretionary enforcement decisions, including the decision to initiate a criminal prosecution or an administrative enforcement action. The report will conclude with a discussion of Congress's authority to restrict executive discretion in the enforcement of federal law.

THE DUAL PURPOSES OF THE TAKE CARE CLAUSE

> [H]e shall take Care that the Laws be faithfully executed...
> U.S. Constitution, Article II, §3

The Take Care Clause would appear to stand for two, at times diametrically opposed propositions—one imposing a "duty" upon the President and the other viewing the Clause as a source of Presidential "power." Primarily, the Take Care Clause has been interpreted as placing an obligation on both the President and those under his supervision to comply with and execute clear statutory directives as enacted by Congress.[16] However, the Supreme Court has also construed the Clause as ensuring Presidential control over the *enforcement* of federal law.[17] As a result, courts generally will not review Presidential enforcement decisions, including the decision of whether to initiate a criminal prosecution or administrative enforcement action in response to a violation of federal law or regulation. The puzzling result is that the Clause has been invoked as forming the constitutional basis for both the President's obligation to enforce the law, and his discretion not to.

The President's Obligation to Follow and Execute the Law

It is beyond dispute that the President plays a significant role in the legislative process. The specific powers enumerated in Article II, §3[18] and Article I, §7[19] of the Constitution, along with the general vesting of "the executive power" in Article II, §1,[20] provide the President with the authority to recommend legislation to Congress, communicate his opposition or support for legislation under consideration,[21] and, ultimately, to either sign legislation that meets his approval, or veto that legislation which "he thinks bad."[22]

It is equally well established, however, that once a bill is enacted into law,[23] the President's legislative role comes to an end and is supplanted by his express constitutional obligation under Article II, §3 to "take Care that the Law[] be faithfully executed."[24] Although there was little discussion of the Clause at the Constitutional Convention, most scholars have agreed that, at a minimum, the Clause represents a repudiation of the royal suspending and dispensing power that had been historically exercised by English monarchs.[25] James Wilson, delegate to the constitutional convention form Pennsylvania, summarized this view in characterizing the Clause as providing the President with the "authority, not to make, or alter, or dispense with the laws, but to execute and act the laws."[26] The executive branch has agreed with this view, acknowledging that "the Supreme Court and the Attorneys General have long interpreted the Take Care Clause as standing for the proposition that the President has no inherent constitutional authority to suspend the enforcement of the laws, particularly of statutes."[27] The Clause would appear then to prevent the President from simply disregarding or suspending laws enacted by Congress.

Today, the Take Care Clause makes a significant contribution to the separation of powers. The constitutionally created distinction between the "faithful" execution of the law under Article II, and the "finely wrought" process for the creation of law under Article I §4, operates as a clear demarcation of the legitimate powers and responsibilities of both the President and Congress in our constitutional system.[28] Just as Congress may neither enforce the laws nor improperly intrude into the President's execution of the same, the President and his subordinates may not create law by unilaterally disregarding, amending, or repealing a validly enacted statute.[29] The ultimate power to legislate is a power possessed solely by Congress, and to permit the President the freedom to suspend, amend, or disregard laws of his choosing would be to "clothe" the executive branch with the power of lawmaking.[30]

A long line of Supreme Court precedent indicates the Court's consistent view that the Take Care Clause imposes a "duty" or "obligation" upon the President to ensure that executive branch officials obey Congress's commands, and, additionally, that the Clause does not provide the President with the authority to frustrate legal requirements imposed by law. The notion that the President and executive branch officers must "faithfully" implement and execute the law can be seen as early as the seminal case of *Marbury v. Madison* in 1803.[31] Although *Marbury* is best known for Chief Justice John Marshall's discussion of the Supreme Court's power of "judicial review"—the authority of the Court to invalidate laws it determines to be unconstitutional—the case also contains strong language relating to the obligation of executive branch officials to comply with the law.

In the final hours of his Presidency, John Adams had appointed William Marbury to serve as Justice of the Peace for the District of Columbia. Marbury's commission, however, was never delivered, and upon assuming office President Thomas Jefferson instructed Secretary of State James Madison to withhold the commission, thus denying Marbury the position. Marbury filed suit, asking the Supreme Court to compel Madison to deliver the commission as, Marbury argued, was required by law. Although the Supreme Court determined that it lacked jurisdiction to hear the case and therefore did not compel Madison to take any action, Chief Justice Marshall nonetheless established that when an executive officer fails to perform a "specific duty [] assigned by law," the courts may enforce the obligation through a writ of mandamus.[32] The *Marbury* opinion recognized Congress's authority to impose specific duties upon executive branch officials by law, as well as the official's corresponding obligation to execute the congressional directive. The general rule established in *Marbury* had limits, however; the Chief Justice drew a clear distinction between the enforceability of ministerial or mandatory requirements—which were subject to judicial enforcement—and political acts involving either statutory or constitutional discretion—which were not.[33]

The Supreme Court's most forceful articulation of the President's obligation to execute the law came thirty years later in *Kendall v. United States ex rel. Stokes*.[34] In *Kendall*, a federal law directed the Postmaster General to provide back pay to a group of mail carrier contractors in an amount determined by the Solicitor of the Treasury. The Postmaster General, apparently at the express direction of the President, refused to pay the amount that the Solicitor had found owing. The Supreme Court, viewing the Postmaster General's duty to pay the full amount as ministerial rather than discretionary, held that the President had no authority to direct the Postmaster's performance of his statutory obligation.[35] Where Congress has imposed upon an executive officer a valid duty, the Court declared "the duty and responsibility grow out of and are subject to the control of the law, and not to the direction of the President."[36] Any interpretation of the Constitution that characterized the obligation of an executive branch official to execute the law as arising from the direction of the President alone, and not as arising from the law itself, would "cloth[e] the President with a power entirely to control the legislation of Congress, and paralyze the administration of justice."[37] "This is a doctrine," the majority held "that cannot receive the sanction of this court."[38]

Perhaps the most significant aspect of the *Kendall* opinion was its repudiation of the government's assertion that the Take Care Clause constituted a source of presidential power. The Court plainly rejected this argument, holding that the Clause could *not* be relied upon as a basis for noncompliance with the law. "To contend that the obligation imposed on the President to see the laws faithfully executed implies a power to forbid their execution," the Court held, "is a novel construction of the Constitution, and entirely inadmissible."[39] The legal reasoning in *Kendall* has long been cited as refuting any asserted presidential power to block the execution of validly enacted statutes.

The Supreme Court reinforced the Constitution's clear distinction between Congress's role in the creation of the law and the President's role in the execution of the law in *Youngstown Sheet & Tube Co. v. Sawyer*.[40] In *Youngstown*, the Court heard a challenge to an Executive Order issued by President Harry Truman directing the Secretary of Commerce to seize various steel mills in an effort to avert the detrimental effect a potential workers' strike would have on the prosecution of the Korean conflict. The Court invalidated the President's directive, holding that neither the Constitution nor any statutory delegation from Congress authorized such an order. The majority opinion was based chiefly on the proposition that the Constitution limits the President's "functions in the lawmaking process" to recommending laws he supports, vetoing laws he opposes, and executing laws that have been enacted by Congress.[41] "In the framework of our Constitution," wrote Justice Black, "the President's power to see that the laws be faithfully executed refutes the idea that he is to be a lawmaker."[42] Justice Jackson's influential concurring opinion likewise concluded that "the Executive, except for recommendation and veto, has no legislative power."[43]

The legal reasoning espoused in *Marbury*, *Kendall*, and *Youngstown* is buttressed by the judicial response to an illustrative conflict in which President Richard Nixon claimed the authority to disregard congressional enactments. Beginning in 1972, President Nixon asserted the authority to decline to spend or obligate appropriated funds in order to reduce public spending and to negate programs established by congressional legislation.[44] Termed an "impoundment," the legal justification for Nixon's policy was claimed to have derived from the Take Care Clause. Most of the courts that reviewed the matter rejected the declared authority, holding—generally on statutory grounds—that neither the President nor the agency heads involved had discretion as to whether to spend appropriated funds.[45] To permit such an action would be to allow a President to substitute his policy choices on spending for those established by congressional appropriations. The Supreme Court agreed in *Train v. City of New York,* holding that as a statutory matter the Administrator of the Environmental Protection Agency had no discretion to withhold funds that had been validly appropriated.[46]

The U.S. District Court for the District of Columbia, however, offered a more robust rejection of the impoundments and the President's claimed constitutional authority. In *Local 2677 AFGE v. Phillips,* the district court held that until Congress terminates a program, "historical precedent, logic, and the text of the Constitution itself obligate the [President] to continue to operate [the program] as was intended by the Congress..."[47] The opinion further suggested that were the President's asserted power to be accepted, "no barrier would remain to the executive ignoring any and all Congressional authorizations if he deemed them, no matter how conscientiously, to be contrary to the needs of the nation."[48]

Notwithstanding the Supreme Court's articulation of the President's constitutional responsibility to execute the law, it is important to note that judicial enforcement of that duty is wholly contingent upon the creation of a well-defined statutory mandate or prohibition.[49] Where Congress has legislated broadly, ambiguously, or in a nonobligatory manner, courts are unlikely to command or halt action by either the President or his officials.[50] Absent the creation of a clear duty, "the executive must be allowed to operate freely within the sphere of discretion created for him by that legislation."[51]

The Take Care Clause as Establishing Presidential Control Over Law Enforcement

In addition to establishing the President's obligation to execute the law, the Supreme Court has simultaneously interpreted the Take Care Clause as ensuring presidential control over those who execute and enforce the law.[52] In framing the Clause as establishing a *personal* responsibility in the President, the court has previously invalidated laws that would undermine the President's ability to oversee the execution and enforcement of the law. [53] These principles have grown mainly out of the Court's consideration of the President's appointment and removal power. In *Bowsher v. Synar*, for example, the Court invalidated a law that had delegated executive powers, including the authority to interpret and execute the law, to the Comptroller General—a legislative branch officer removable by Congress.[54] The Court held that "[a] direct congressional role in the removal of officers charged with the execution of the laws ... is inconsistent with separation of powers."[55]

Likewise, in *Buckley v. Valeo*, the Court determined that Congress could not provide itself with the power to appoint members of an independent commission that had been vested, among other powers, with the authority to undertake enforcement actions.[56] In striking down the appointment structure of the Federal Election Commission, the Court held that "a lawsuit is the ultimate remedy for a breach of the law, and it is to the President, and not to Congress, that the Constitution entrusts the responsibility to take care that the laws be faithfully executed."[57]

In *Printz v. U.S,* the Court suggested that vesting state and local officers with the authority to enforce federal law may also intrude upon the President's duty to oversee those that execute the law.[58] Although *Printz* is primarily known as a 10th Amendment case addressing federal intrusion into state sovereignty, the Court also considered the effect the Brady Handgun Violence Prevention Act would have on the President's obligation to "take Care that the Laws be faithfully executed." At issue in *Printz* was a provision of the Act that required the chief law enforcement officers (CLEOs) of state and local governments to conduct background checks to ascertain whether individuals were ineligible to purchase handguns. The Court suggested that the law may impermissibly diminish presidential power, noting:

> The Constitution does not leave to speculation who is to administer the laws enacted by Congress; the President, it says, "shall take Care that the Laws be faithfully executed," personally and through officers whom he appoints...The Brady Act effectively transfers this responsibility to thousands of CLEOs in the 50 States, who are left to implement the program without meaningful Presidential control (if indeed meaningful Presidential control is possible without the power to appoint and remove). The insistence of the Framers upon unity in the Federal Executive—to ensure both vigor and accountability—is well known. That unity would be shattered, and the power of the President would be subject to reduction, if Congress could act as effectively without the President as with him, by simply requiring state officers to execute its laws.[59]

More recently in *Free Enterprise Fund v. PCAOB*, the Supreme Court invalidated a statute that insulated officers of the Public Company Accountability Oversight Board from the President by providing Board members with dual layers of "for cause" removal protections.[60] In the course of striking down the law, the Court cited with approval the holding in *Myers v. U.S.* that the President must retain "general administrative control of those executing the laws," for he cannot "'take Care that the laws be faithfully executed' if he cannot oversee the faithfulness of the officers who execute them."[61]

Whereas the President must be able to oversee those who enforce the law, Presidential control over law enforcement officers need not be absolute. In *Morrison v Olson*, a case upholding a law establishing the office of the Independent Counsel, the Court summarized its removal jurisprudence as ensuring that "Congress does not interfere with the President's exercise of the 'executive power' and his constitutionally appointed duty to 'take care that the laws be faithfully executed' under Article II."[62] However, the opinion then sanctioned Congress's authority to provide a prosecutor with independence from the President by providing the officer with "for cause" removal protections—holding that such protections did *not* "sufficiently deprive[] the

President of control over the independent counsel to interfere impermissibly with his constitutional obligation to ensure the faithful execution of the laws."[63] *Morrison*, which may act as a significant limitation on the exclusivity of executive branch enforcement discretion, will subsequently be discussed in greater detail.

As a corollary to the requirement that the President must retain some level of control over those that enforce the law, the courts have similarly cited the Clause as providing the President and his officers with discretion as to *how* the laws are to be enforced against the general public. This discretion has been considered an essential component of the President's obligation to "discharge his constitutional responsibility to 'take Care that the Laws be faithfully executed.'"[64] It is worth emphasizing, however, that any discretion that may arise from the Take Care Clause would extend only to decisions directly related to the enforcement of federal law upon third parties. At no time has the Court recognized the Clause as a justification for either affirmatively suspending federal law or refusing to comply with explicit mandates or restrictions imposed on the executive branch. Moreover, whether executive enforcement discretion constitutes a presidential "power" or a rule of judicial restraint is an important question, and a crucial one in delineating Congress's authority to restrict that discretion, yet unanswered by the Supreme Court.

The Obama Administration has relied upon enforcement discretion, in both the criminal and administrative context, as the chief legal justification for the previously identified actions and it is to this doctrine that this report now turns.

PROSECUTORIAL DISCRETION AND JUDICIAL RESTRAINT

The judicial branch has traditionally accorded federal prosecutors "broad" latitude in making a range of investigatory and prosecutorial determinations, including when, against whom, and whether to prosecute particular criminal violations of federal law.[65] This doctrine of prosecutorial discretion has a long historical pedigree—the early roots of which can be traced at least to a sixteenth century English common law procedural mechanism known as the *nolle prosequi*.[66] In the early English legal system, criminal prosecutions were generally initiated by private individuals rather than public prosecutors. The *nolle prosequi*, however, allowed the government, generally at the direction of the Crown, to intervene in and terminate a privately initiated criminal action it viewed as "frivolous or in contravention of royal interests."[67] The discretionary device and its principles were later adopted into American common law, permitting prosecutors to avoid prosecutions that were determined to be unwarranted or which the prosecuting authority chose not to pursue.[68]

Notwithstanding this historical background, the modern doctrine of prosecutorial discretion derives more from our constitutional structure than English common law. The exact justification for the doctrine, however, does not appear to have been explicitly established. Generally, courts have characterized prosecutorial discretion as a function of some mixture of constitutional principles, including the separation of powers, the Take Care Clause, and the duties of a prosecutor as an appointee of the President.[69] Regardless of its precise textual source, courts generally will not review discretionary prosecutorial decisions in criminal matters, nor coerce the executive branch to initiate a particular prosecution. Most courts have agreed that judicial review of prosecutorial decisions is generally improper given that the "prosecutorial function, and the discretion that accompanies it, is [] committed by the Constitution to the executive."[70]

Judicial deference to prosecutorial decisions made by federal prosecutors has been justified on the ground that the "decision to prosecute is particularly ill-suited to judicial review."[71] The courts have repeatedly acknowledged that these types of discretionary decisions involve the consideration of factors—such as the strength of evidence, deterrence value, available resources, and existing enforcement priorities—"not readily susceptible to the kind of analysis the courts are competent to undertake."[72] Indeed, "[f]ew subjects are less adapted to judicial review than the exercise by the Executive of his discretion in deciding when and whether to institute criminal proceedings, or what precise charge shall be made, or whether to dismiss a proceeding once brought."[73]

A core aspect of prosecutorial discretion would appear to be the decision to initiate a criminal prosecution.[74] As a result, judicial hesitance to review prosecutorial decisions is perhaps at its peak when the government chooses not to prosecute. The Supreme Court issued one of its strongest pronouncements of this principle in *U.S. v. Nixon*, proclaiming that "the Executive Branch has exclusive authority and absolute discretion to decide whether to prosecute a case."[75] Although the Court did not elaborate on the statement, other lower courts have adopted similar lines of reasoning. For example, a strong statement of judicial restraint was issued in the oft cited case of *United States v. Cox*, in which the U.S. Court of Appeals for the Fifth Circuit (Fifth Circuit) held that a district court could not compel a U.S. Attorney to sign an indictment returned by the grand jury.[76] The court held that as an

> officer of the executive department...[the prosecutor] exercises a discretion as to whether or not there shall be a prosecution in a particular case. It follows as an incident of the constitutional separation of powers, that the courts are not to interfere with the free exercise of the discretionary powers of the attorneys of the United States in their control over criminal prosecutions.[77]

This principle was further exemplified by the U.S. Court of Appeals for the Second Circuit (Second Circuit) in *Inmates of Attica Correctional Facility v. Rockefeller*.[78] In that case, prison inmates brought suit against the U.S. Attorney for the Western District of New York for his failure to take any action against government officials following the suppression of the Attica prison revolt that resulted in the deaths of 32 inmates. The plaintiffs sought a mandamus order, directing the U.S. Attorney to "investigate, arrest, and prosecute" those state officials who committed federal criminal civil rights violations.[79] The court dismissed the claim, holding that "federal courts have traditionally *and, to our knowledge, uniformly* refrained from overturning...discretionary decisions of federal prosecuting authorities not to prosecute..."[80] The court noted that this "judicial reluctance" and the "traditional judicial aversion to compelling prosecutions" is grounded in the constitutional separation of powers as well as the practical consideration that "the manifold imponderables which enter into the prosecutor's decision to prosecute or not to prosecute make the choice not readily amendable to judicial supervision."[81]

In its view, the executive branch has asserted that it must maintain absolute control over prosecutorial decisions, concluding specifically that "because the essential core of the President's constitutional responsibility is the duty to enforce the laws, the Executive Branch has exclusive authority to initiate and prosecute actions to enforce the laws adopted by Congress."[82] The DOJ has also asserted a "corollary" proposition, "that neither the Judicial nor Legislative Branches may directly interfere with the prosecutorial discretion of the Executive by directing the Executive Branch to prosecute particular individuals."[83]

While prosecutorial discretion is broad, it is not "unfettered."[84] Indeed, the government "cannot cloak constitutional violations under the guise of prosecutorial discretion and expect the federal courts simply to look the other way."[85] For example, in discussing the scope of the executive branch's discretion, courts have repeatedly noted that the determination as to whether to prosecute may not be based upon "race, religion, or other arbitrary classification."[86] Nor may an exercise of prosecutorial discretion infringe individual constitutional rights.[87] Where prosecutions (or other enforcement actions) are based upon impermissible factors "the judiciary must protect against unconstitutional deprivations."[88] This principle was evident in *Yick Wo v. Hopkins*, where the Supreme Court found that prosecutors' practice of enforcing a state law prohibiting the operation of laundries against only persons of Chinese descent ran afoul of the Equal Protection Clause.[89] In practice, however, defendants generally find it difficult to maintain a claim of selective prosecution. Courts generally require defendants to introduce "clear evidence" displacing the presumption that the prosecutor has acted lawfully.[90]

In addition to reviewing decisions that violate individual constitutional rights, courts may also choose to review prosecutorial decisions for compliance with express statutory requirements. In *Nader v Saxbe*, a case involving nonenforcement of the Federal Corrupt Practices Act, the U.S. Court of Appeals for the District of Columbia Circuit (D.C. Circuit) suggested that "the exercise of prosecutorial discretion, like the exercise of Executive discretion generally, is subject to *statutory* and constitutional limits enforceable through judicial review."[91] Although dismissing the case for lack of standing, the D.C. Circuit rejected the district court's determination that "prosecutorial decision-making is wholly immune from judicial review."[92] Therefore, it would appear that where Congress has explicitly established a statutory framework under which prosecutions are to take place, and as a result altered the traditional scope of prosecutorial discretion, "the judiciary has the responsibility of assuring that the purpose and intent of congressional enactments are not negated..."[93] Under these rare circumstances, courts may elect to review prosecutorial decisions—including the decision of whether to initiate a criminal prosecution— to ensure compliance with federal law.

However, courts have been reluctant to read criminal statutes as establishing the type of framework necessary to withdraw the executive's discretion to decide whether to initiate a prosecution, instead requiring clear and unambiguous evidence of Congress's intent to withdraw traditional prosecutorial discretion. For example, in *Powell v Katzenbach,* the D.C. Circuit dismissed a challenge to the Attorney' General's failure to prosecute a national bank for certain criminal violations.[94] After assuming, "without deciding, that where Congress has withdrawn all discretion from the prosecutor by special legislation, a court might be empowered to force prosecutions in some circumstances," the circuit court determined "the language of [the provision in question] and its legislative history fail to disclose a congressional intent to alter the traditional scope of the prosecutor's discretion."[95] Moreover, both the U.S. Court of appeals for the Fourth Circuit (Fourth Circuit) and the U.S. District Court for the District of Columbia have held that language in the federal civil rights statutes stating that U.S. Attorneys are "authorized *and required to institute prosecutions* against all persons violating" certain provisions of the Civil Rights Act[96] similarly failed to "strip" federal prosecutors of "their normal prosecutorial discretion."[97] The Fourth Circuit specifically found the use of the word "require" to be "insufficient to evince a broad congressional purpose to bar the exercise of executive discretion in the prosecution of federal civil rights crimes."[98] As a result, the court determined that it was "unnecessary to decide whether, if Congress were by explicit direction and guidelines to remove all prosecutorial discretion with respect to certain crimes or in certain circumstances we would properly direct that a prosecution be undertaken."[99]

The separation of powers concerns that would derive from a law that unambiguously and expressly sought to remove prosecutorial discretion and compel criminal prosecutions will be explored in greater detail *infra.*[100]

JUDICIAL REVIEW OF ADMINISTRATIVE NONENFORCEMENT

Agency civil enforcement decisions in the *administrative* context "share[] to some extent the characteristics of the decision of a prosecutor" in the *criminal* context.[101] This freedom in setting enforcement priorities, allocating resources, and making specific strategic enforcement decisions— including the decision to initiate an enforcement action— is commonly described as "administrative enforcement discretion." Whether this form of enforcement discretion enjoys the same constitutional footing as prosecutorial discretion is not entirely clear. Indeed, the judicial reluctance to review agency enforcement decisions would appear to arise as much from the Administrative Procedure Act (APA) as it does from the Take Care Clause.

Although the APA establishes a general presumption that all final agency decisions are subject to judicial review, it also specifically precludes from judicial consideration any agency action that is "committed to agency discretion by law."[102] A decision is generally considered "committed to agency discretion" when a reviewing court would have "no law to apply" in evaluating the determination.[103] Consistent with this framework, and in light of the traditional discretion exercised by agencies in enforcing statutes they administer, courts generally will not review discretionary agency enforcement decisions.[104] These discretionary activities may include any range of actions and decisions taken throughout the investigative and enforcement process, including, but not limited to, the imposition of penalties or the initiation of an agency investigation, prosecution, adjudication, lawsuit, or audit.[105]

In situations where an agency *refrains* from bringing an enforcement action, courts have historically been cautious in reviewing the agency determination—generally holding that these nonenforcement decisions are "committed to agency discretion" and therefore not subject to judicial review under the APA.[106] The seminal case on this topic is *Heckler v. Chaney*, a Supreme Court decision in which death row inmates challenged the Food and Drug Administration's refusal to initiate an enforcement action to block the use of certain drugs in lethal injection.[107] In rejecting the challenge, the Supreme Court held that "an agency's decision not to prosecute or enforce...is a decision generally committed to an agency's absolute discretion."[108] The Court noted that agency enforcement decisions, involve a "complicated balancing of a number of factors which are peculiarly within [the agency's] expertise" including,

> whether agency resources are best spent on this violation or another, whether the agency is likely to succeed if it acts, whether the particular enforcement action requested best fits the agency's overall policies, and, indeed, whether the agency has enough resources to undertake the action at all. An agency generally cannot act against each technical violation of the statute it is charged with enforcing.[109]

Agencies, the Court reasoned, are "far better equipped" to evaluate "the many variables involved in the proper ordering of its priorities" than are the courts.[110] Consistent with this deferential view, the *Heckler* opinion proceeded to establish the standard for the reviewability of agency nonenforcement decisions, holding that an "agency's decision not to take enforcement action should be *presumed immune from judicial review*."[111]

However, the Court also clearly indicated that the presumption against judicial review of agency nonenforcement decisions may be overcome in a variety of specific situations.[112] For purposes of this report, two identified exceptions necessitate significant discussion. First, a court may review an agency nonenforcement determination "where the substantive statute has provided guidelines for the agency to follow in exercising its enforcement powers."[113] In such a situation, Congress has supplied the court with "law to apply" in reviewing the agency decision. Second, the Court suggested that judicial review of nonenforcement may be appropriate when an agency has "'consciously and expressly adopted a general policy' that is so extreme as to amount to an abdication of its statutory responsibilities."[114] Due presumably to standing limitations, lower federal courts have only rarely had opportunity to clarify these exceptions to *Heckler's* presumption of non-reviewability of nonenforcement decisions.[115]

Statutory Guidelines

The *Heckler* opinion specifically recognized Congress's authority to curtail an agency's ability to exercise enforcement discretion "either by setting substantive priorities, or by otherwise circumscribing an agency's power to discriminate among issues or cases it will pursue."[116] Congress may, for instance, choose to remove an agency's discretion by indicating "an intent to circumscribe agency enforcement discretion" and "provid[ing] meaningful standards for defining the limits of that discretion."[117] In this manner Congress overrides the inherent discretion possessed by the agencies in the enforcement of federal law and provides a reviewing court with a standard upon which to review the agency inaction. The Court succinctly articulated the principle in *Heckler*:

> If [Congress] has indicated an intent to circumscribe agency enforcement discretion, and has provided meaningful standards for defining the limits of that discretion, there is "law to apply" under [the APA] and courts may require that the agency follow that law; if it has not, then an agency refusal to institute proceedings is a decision "committed to agency discretion by law" within the meaning of that section.[118]

Although the exercise of agency discretion may therefore be influenced by congressional controls, it would appear that Congress's intent to curtail the agency enforcement discretion must be made explicit, as courts are hesitant to imply such limitations.[119]

In applying this standard, the *Heckler* opinion held that the FFDCA had not curtailed the FDA's discretion in a manner sufficient to allow the court to review the agency's nonenforcement determination. The FFDCA provided only that the Secretary was "authorized to conduct examinations and investigations;" and not that he was required to do so.[120] Moreover, the Court determined that the FFDCA's requirement that any person who violates the Act "shall be imprisoned...or fined," could *not* be read to mandate that the FDA initiate an enforcement action in response to every violation.[121] The FFDCA's prohibition on certain conduct, although framed in mandatory terms, was insufficient to permit review of nonenforcement absent additional language delineating how and when the agency was to respond to violations. "The Act's enforcement provisions," held the Court "thus commit complete discretion to the Secretary to decide how and when they should be exercised."[122]

In his concurrence, Justice Brennan identified the potential consequences of the majority's position and attempted to narrow the scope of the opinion, writing that agencies should not feel "free to disregard legislative direction in the statutory scheme that the agency administers."[123] Brennan emphasized that the presumption against reviewability applied only to the "individual, isolated nonenforcement decisions" that "must be made by hundreds of agencies each day."[124] "Absent some indication of congressional intent to the contrary," Brennan found it reasonable to believe that Congress did not intend the courts to review "such mundane matters."[125]

Justice Brennan's more limited reasoning had carried the day in the pre-*Heckler* case of *Dunlop v. Bachowski*.[126] In *Dunlop*, a union member challenged the Secretary of Labor's refusal to bring an enforcement action to set aside a union election. The Labor-Management Reporting and Disclosure Act (L-MRDA) provides that upon the filing of a complaint, "[t]he Secretary shall investigate such complaint and, if he finds probable cause to believe that a violation... has occurred...he shall...bring a civil action..."[127] Brennan's majority opinion rejected the agency's argument that the Secretary's determination of whether to bring a civil action was an unreviewable exercise of administrative discretion. In doing so, the Court did not itself address the enforcement discretion question, but rather stated its agreement with the appellate court's conclusion that "[a]lthough the Secretary's decision to bring suit bears some similarity to the decision to commence a criminal prosecution, the principle of absolute prosecutorial discretion is not applicable to the facts of this case." [128]

The appellate court identified two reasons for this conclusion. First, the court found that enforcement discretion in the civil context should be limited to cases which, "like criminal prosecutions, involve the vindication of societal or governmental interests, rather than the protection of individual rights."[129] Second, the court found the "most convincing reasoning" for reviewability of the Secretary's decision was that in criminal cases, a prosecutor generally must balance "considerations that are 'beyond the judicial capacity to supervise.'"[130] To the contrary, the court found the "factors to be considered by the secretary" under the L-MRDA to be "more limited and clearly defined."[131] The court determined that the statute:

> provides that after investigating a complaint, he must determine whether there is probable cause to believe that violations of § 481 have occurred affecting the outcome of the election. Where a complaint is meritorious and no settlement has been reached which would remedy the violations found to exist, the language and purpose of § 402(b) indicate that Congress intended the Secretary to file suit. Thus, apart from the possibility of settlement, the Secretary's decision whether to bring suit depends on a rather straightforward factual determination, and we see nothing in the nature of that task that places the Secretary's decision 'beyond the judicial capacity to supervise.'[132]

The language held to override the presumption against review of agency nonenforcement in *Dunlop* contained an express trigger for an enforcement action. The Secretary, however, retained discretion in determining whether the precondition (whether there was probable cause to believe a violation had occurred) was met.[133]

The Supreme Court confirmed the continued validity of *Dunlop* in *Heckler*, but distinguished the two decisions, holding that unlike the FFDCA, the L-MRDA "quite clearly withdrew discretion from the agency and provided guidelines for exercise of its enforcement power."[134]

Federal statutes, unlike the L-MRDA, that do not contain language defining how and when the agency is to exercise its enforcement discretion, even when framed in mandatory terms, generally have not been held to override agency enforcement discretion. As previously discussed, a congressional command that an agency "shall enforce" a particular statute, without additional guidelines as to the circumstances under which enforcement is to occur, is generally insufficient to permit review of a nonenforcement decision. The *Heckler* court suggested as much, noting that it could not "attribute such a sweeping meaning" to the type of mandatory language that was commonly found in federal law.[135]

A Florida district court applied this reasoning in its review of a statute commanding that "the provisions of [the Endangered Species Act (ESA)] and any regulations or permits issued pursuant thereto *shall* be enforced by the Secretary."[136] Citing to *Heckler*, the court held that the provision "plainly does not mandate an impossibility—i.e., the Service to pursue to the fullest each and every possible violation of the ESA or permits thereunder."[137] Moreover, the ESA did not "provide criteria or guidelines charting a process the Service shall use to investigate possible noncompliance."[138]

The U.S. District Court for the Northern District of Texas applied *Heckler* and *Dunlop* in a recent challenge to the Secretary of Homeland Security's exercise of administrative enforcement discretion in the granting of "deferred action"— the name given to one type of relief from removal whereby immigration officials agree to forego taking action against an individual for a specified time frame—under the DACA memorandum.[139] In *Crane v. Napolitano*, Immigration and Customs Enforcement (ICE) agents asserted that the Secretary's directive was in violation of the Immigration and Nationality Act (INA), which, the plaintiffs argued, "requires" ICE officers to initiate a removal proceeding if they encounter an unlawfully present alien who is not "clearly and beyond a doubt entitled to be admitted."[140]

Section 1225(b)(2)(A) of the INA provides that if an "examining immigration officer determines that an alien seeking admission is not clearly and beyond a doubt entitled to be admitted, the alien shall be detained for a [removal] proceeding..."[141] In response to a motion for a preliminary injunction, the district court determined that the INA established an obligation for officers to initiate a removal proceeding against any alien whom the officer determines is not "clearly and beyond a doubt entitled to be admitted."[142] The court held that judicial review of the agency nonenforcement policy was appropriate because the INA "provides clearly defined factors for when inspecting immigration officers are required to initiate removal proceedings against an arriving alien, just as the statute at issue in *Dunlop* provided certain clearly defined factors for when the Secretary of Labor was required to file a civil action."[143] The district court ultimately dismissed the case, however, holding that the employment related claims asserted by the ICE agents were within the exclusive jurisdiction of the Merit Systems Protection Board and, therefore, not properly before the court. [144]

The above cases would appear to establish the proposition that agency nonenforcement decisions are presumptively unreviewable exercises of administrative discretion. However, when Congress removes or restricts that discretion, by expressly providing "guidelines" or "meaningful standards" for the manner in which the agency may exercise its enforcement powers, the presumption of nonreviewability may be overcome. Whether Congress has provided sufficient guidelines is difficult to determine. For example, establishing that certain conduct constitutes a violation of law and then authorizing an agency to enforce that law, or even establishing that the agency "shall" enforce the law or is "required" to enforce the law, would appear to be insufficient to overcome the *Heckler* presumption. However, where Congress clearly imposes criteria, considerations, standards, or guidelines on the agency's exercise of its enforcement discretion (i.e., when, or how the agency is to take enforcement actions) or establishes clear conditions to trigger enforcement actions, it would appear that courts may review whether a nonenforcement decision contravenes the statutory framework.

If a court finds that a statute permits review of an agency nonenforcement decision, it would appear that that decision will be evaluated for compliance with statutory requirements under the "arbitrary and capricious" test established in §706 of the APA.[145] In *Dunlop*, the Court was careful to make clear that in such a situation, the reviewing court may not "substitute its judgment for the decision of the [agency] not to bring suit."[146] The court's role is limited to determining "whether or not the discretion, which still remains in the [agency], has been exercised in a manner that is neither arbitrary nor capricious."[147] In order to conduct this review, a court may require that the agency provide a statement of reasons as to why the nonenforcement decision was made that addressed "both the grounds of decision and the essential facts upon which the [agency's] inferences are based."[148] The court can then evaluate whether the agency's decision was "reached for an impermissible reason or for no reason at all."[149] To the contrary, "if the court concludes there is a rational and defensible basis [for the agency's] determination, then that should be an end of [the] matter, for it is not the function of the Court to determine whether or not the case should be brought or what its outcome would be."[150]

Abdication of Statutory Responsibilities

In *Heckler*, the Supreme Court also suggested that the presumption against the review of nonenforcement decisions may be overcome if the agency has "'consciously and expressly adopted a general policy' that is so extreme as to amount to an abdication of its statutory responsibilities."[151] The Court, however, was unclear as to whether such an agency policy would in fact be reviewable, stating only that "[a]lthough we express no opinion on whether such decisions would be unreviewable under [the APA], we note that in those situations the statute conferring authority on the agency might indicate that such decisions were not "committed to agency discretion."[152]

In raising the "statutory abdication" argument, the Court cited to *Adams v. Richardson*, a decision from the D.C. Circuit.[153] *Adams* involved a challenge to the Secretary of Health, Education, and Welfare's (HEW) failure to enforce Title VI of the Civil rights Act of 1964.[154] The Act "authorizes and directs" federal agencies to ensure that federal financial assistance is not provided to segregated educational institutions.[155] The district court had rejected the Secretary's assertion that the law provided federal agencies with "absolute discretion" with respect to whether to take action to terminate funding, holding that the agency has "the duty of accomplishing the purposes of the statute through administrative enforcement proceedings or by other legal means."[156] The district court ordered the agency to commence enforcement proceedings against certain school districts within a specified time period.[157]

The D.C. Circuit affirmed the district court decision in language characteristic of the "statutory guidelines" exception, holding that "Title VI not only requires the agency to enforce the Act, but also sets forth specific enforcement procedures."[158] The court distinguished the *Adams* nonenforcement scenario from traditional exercises of enforcement discretion, noting that in past cases, Congress had not enacted "specific legislation requiring particular action."[159] The court appeared to then give great weight to the breadth of the Secretary's nonenforcement, noting:

> More significantly, this suit is not brought to challenge HEW's decisions with regard to a few school districts in the course of a generally effective enforcement program. To the contrary, appellants allege that HEW has consciously and expressly adopted a general policy which is in effect an abdication of its statutory duty.[160]

The court determined that HEW had consistently and unsuccessfully relied on voluntary compliance as a means of enforcing Title VI without resorting to the more formal and effective enforcement procedures available to the agency. This "consistent failure" was a "dereliction of duty reviewable in the courts."[161]

Although arguably applicable to any "general policy" of nonenforcement, the *Adams* opinion may be limited to certain types of enforcement. In reaching its conclusion the court stressed the "nature of the relationship between the agency and the institutions in question."[162] The court noted that:

> HEW is actively supplying segregated institutions with federal funds, contrary to the expressed purposes of Congress. It is one thing to say the Justice Department lacks the resources necessary to locate and prosecute every civil rights violator; it is quite another to say HEW may affirmatively continue to channel federal funds to defaulting schools. The anomaly of this latter assertion fully supports the conclusion that Congress's clear statement of an affirmative enforcement duty should not be discounted.[163]

As such, it is not clear that the *Adams* exception would apply with equal force to more traditional enforcement actions—such as those that require the expenditure of significant agency resources in investigating and penalizing members of the public for violations of law.

Given the sparse case law associated with this exception, it is difficult to assess what level of nonenforcement constitutes an "abdication of statutory responsibilities." Presumably, if an agency announced that it would no longer enforce a provision of law against any individual at any time, regardless of the nature of the violation, a court would likely be willing to review the policy.[164] The Fifth Circuit, however, has stated that merely "inadequate" enforcement is insufficient to overcome the *Heckler* presumption of nonreviewability.[165] In *Texas v. United States*, the state of Texas sued the United States arguing that the Attorney General had failed to control immigration as dictated by the INA, and that the failure to enforce the immigration laws had resulted in substantial costs to the state.[166] With respect to the enforcement claim, the court rejected "out-ofhand the State's contention that the federal defendants' alleged systemic failure to control immigration is so extreme as to constitute a reviewable abdication of duty."[167] In holding that nonenforcement decisions are not subject to judicial review, the court concluded:

> The State does not contend that federal defendants are doing nothing to enforce the immigration laws or that they have consciously decided to abdicate their enforcement responsibilities. Real or perceived *inadequate* enforcement of immigration laws does not constitute a reviewable abdication of duty.[168]

Whether limited nonenforcement policies— for instance if an agency announced that it will *delay* enforcement of a particular provision for a specified period of time—could also be subject to review would appear to be less clear. For example, in *Schering Corp. v. Heckler*, the D.C. Circuit held that the FDA decision not to pursue an enforcement action against a drug manufacturer for a specific period of time fell "squarely within the confines of *Chaney*" and was therefore not reviewable.[169] In that case, the FDA had reached a settlement with an animal drug manufacturer in which the agency had agreed not to "initiate any enforcement action...for a period of 18 months."[170] A rival drug manufacturer brought a claim seeking a declaration that the settlement was invalid. The court dismissed the claim, holding that there was no "policy or pattern of nonenforcment that amounts to 'an abdication of its statutory responsibilities,'" and that the agency decision to hold enforcement in "abeyance" while it considered its position was a "paradigm case of enforcement discretion."[171] It should be noted that as a general matter, agency delays are notoriously difficult to enforce, even in situations where Congress has established a clear statutory deadline for mandatory action.[172]

Distinguishing Individual Nonenforcement Decisions From Nonenforcement Policies

In light of the standards established in *Heckler* and other cases, it would appear that, absent explicit statutory language, challenges to particular prosecutorial or agency nonenforcement decisions are unlikely to meet with much success. Courts have made clear that these decisions are generally committed to the agency's or the prosecutor's discretion and are not subject to judicial review. However, the mere invocation of prosecutorial or enforcement discretion is not "to be treated as a magical incantation which automatically provides a shield for arbitrariness."[173]

It would appear that courts may be more willing to grant review of established agency policies of nonenforcement than more traditional, case-by-case, individual enforcement decisions. Justice Brennan emphasized this point in his *Heckler* concurrence, noting that that the presumption against reviewability applied only to "individual, isolated nonenforcement decisions."[174] Similarly, in *Crowley Caribbean Transportation v. Pena*, the D.C. Circuit made a clear distinction between "single-shot nonenforcement decisions" on one hand, and "an agency's statement of a general enforcement policy" on the other.[175] The court determined that review of an agency's "general enforcement policy" was reviewable where the agency had 1) "expressed the policy as a formal regulation," 2) "articulated [the policy] in some form of universal policy statement," or 3) otherwise "[laid] out a general policy delineating the boundary between enforcement and nonenforcement" that "purport[s] to speak to a broad class of parties."[176] The court articulated its reasons for finding review of general enforcement, or nonenforcement policies to be appropriate as follows:

> By definition, expressions of broad enforcement policies are abstracted from the particular combinations of facts the agency would encounter in individual enforcement proceedings. As general statements, they are more likely to be direct interpretations of the commands of the substantive statute rather than the sort of mingled assessments of fact, policy, and law that drive an individual enforcement decision and that are, as *Chaney* recognizes, peculiarly within the agency's expertise and discretion. Second, an agency's pronouncement of a broad policy against enforcement poses special risks that it 'has consciously and expressly adopted a general policy that is so extreme as to amount to an abdication of its statutory responsibilities,' a situation in which the normal presumption of nonreviewability may be inappropriate. Finally, an agency will generally present a clearer (and more easily reviewable) statement of its reasons for acting when formally articulating a broadly applicable enforcement policy, whereas such statements in the context of individual decisions to forego enforcement tend to be cursory, ad hoc, or post hoc.[177]

Other cases similarly support the notion that courts are more willing to review nonenforcement policies than individual enforcement-based decisions in both the criminal and administrative contexts. In *Nader v. Saxbe*, the D.C. Circuit drew a clear distinction between judicial review of discretionary enforcement decisions, and judicial review of compliance with "statutory and constitutional limits to" those decisions.[178] *Nader* was a suit in which a nonprofit corporation asked the court to compel the Attorney General to initiate criminal prosecutions under the Federal Corrupt Practices Act, a law that required presidential candidates and committees supporting presidential candidates to file reports on campaign contributions and expenditures. The plaintiffs argued that despite numerous allegations of violations of the law, DOJ had adopted a policy, based on prosecutorial discretion, to only respond to violations referred by the Clerk of the House or the Secretary of the Senate. Although the court found that the plaintiffs lacked standing to bring the claim, it nevertheless determined that "established precedents" do not "necessarily foreclose judicial review of [nonenforcement] policies."179 The court then drew a clear distinction between the review of individual enforcement decisions and the review of broad nonenforcement policies:

> The instant complaint does not ask the court to assume the essentially Executive function of deciding whether a particular alleged violator should be prosecuted. Rather, the complaint seeks a conventionally judicial determination of whether certain fixed policies allegedly followed by the Justice Department and the United States Attorney's office lie outside the constitutional and statutory limits of "prosecutorial discretion."[180]

One reason a court may be more receptive to reviewing a nonenforcement policy, as opposed to an individual nonenforcement decision, could relate to the remedy that would ultimately be provided if the court reached a decision favorable to the plaintiffs. The remedy to an individual nonenforcement decision would likely be a court order, perhaps in the form of a writ of mandamus, directing the agency to initiate an enforcement action. Mandamus is an "extraordinary remedy reserved for extraordinary circumstances," and will generally only be issued where there is a violation of a "clear duty to act."[181] While courts have granted mandamus to compel an agency to issue a rule where Congress has provided an explicit deadline, courts are generally loathe to order enforcement actions.[182] Indeed, the D.C. Circuit has held in the criminal context that "it is well settled that the question of whether and when prosecution is to be instituted is within the discretion of the Attorney General. Mandamus will not lie to control the exercise of this discretion."[183] To the contrary, a court may have greater flexibility in crafting a remedy to an invalid agency nonenforcement policy. For instance, if a reviewing court found the agency policy to be inconsistent with the existing statutory framework, the court may simply invalidate the policy, or direct the agency to reconsider its policy, without necessarily taking additional steps or directing the agency to take any specific action.

This line of reasoning was evident in the U.S. Court of Appeals for the Eleventh Circuit opinion of *Smith v. Meese*.[184] *Meese* involved a claim by black voters and elected officials challenging "a policy and pattern of investigatory and prosecutory decisions," including the nonenforcement of federal civil rights laws, that allegedly had the effect of depriving the plaintiffs of their constitutional rights.[185] In holding that the separation of powers was not threatened by judicial review of the prosecutorial decisions, the court found it "important to note" that rather than being "asked to block or require the prosecution of any individual" the plaintiffs had instead "asked the federal court to order the defendants to stop following a deliberate policy of discriminatory investigations and prosecutions."[186] The court went on to address the type of remedy that a court may be likely to grant in a challenge to nonenforcement, suggesting that

> It is unlikely that the appropriate remedy would be for the district court to enjoin all voting fraud prosecutions or to require prosecutions of all possible election crimes. Instead, it is likely that the district court would order the defendants to make prosecutorial decisions based on *constitutional* factors, instead of targeting one race or one political party for investigation.[187]

The Executive branch likewise acknowledges that "the individual prosecutorial decision is distinguishable from instances in which courts have reviewed the legality of general executive branch policies."[188]

THE SEPARATION OF POWERS: CONGRESSIONAL AUTHORITY TO CURTAIL ENFORCEMENT DISCRETION

As the foregoing discussion makes clear, there is a default presumption that the executive branch has discretion in making a wide range of decisions relating to the discharge of its duty to enforce federal law. Congress, however, may alter the default rule by explicitly guiding or restricting the exercise of that discretion through statute. The Supreme Court has stated quite bluntly that "[a]ll constitutional questions aside, it is for *Congress* to determine how the rights which it creates shall be enforced."[189] In the administrative context, this principle was reflected in *Heckler*, where the Court expressly held that Congress may establish "guidelines for the agency to follow in exercising its enforcement powers" and the "Congress may limit an agency's exercise of enforcement power if it wishes, either by setting substantive priorities, or by otherwise circumscribing an agency's power to discriminate among issues or cases it will pursue."[190] Thus, Congress may restrain administrative enforcement discretion by statute, and enact laws that reduce agency officials' freedom in making enforcement, and indeed nonenforcement, decisions.

These principles arguably apply with equal force in the criminal context.[191] Indeed, a pair of early Supreme Court cases suggest that the exercise of prosecutorial discretion must conform to statutory restrictions.[192] In *U.S. v. Morgan* the Supreme Court considered whether a Department of Agriculture hearing was a required condition precedent to a DOJ criminal prosecution under the Pure Food and Drug Act.[193] Under the law, if agency officials determined that a violation had occurred, the federal prosecutor was obliged "to cause appropriate proceedings to be commenced and prosecuted."[194] Although the case did not focus on whether the law mandated prosecutions, the court nonetheless stated in dicta that the law created a "condition where the district attorney is *compelled* to prosecute without delay."[195] In noting that the statute "compels [the prosecutor] to act" and that " he...is bound to accept the finding of the Department," the Court made no mention of prosecutorial discretion or the separation of powers.[196]

The Court suggested a similar congressional role in influencing criminal prosecutorial decisions in the *Confiscation Cases*.[197] In that decision, which has been viewed as "one of the canonical statements of executive authority over prosecution," the Supreme Court nonetheless suggested in dicta that the executive branch's control over the termination of criminal prosecutions may be subject to limits imposed by statute.[198] Although the case upheld the federal prosecutor's discretion to dismiss a forfeiture suit, the Court qualified that discretion by suggesting that "public prosecutions...are within the exclusive direction of the district attorney *except in cases where it is otherwise provided in some act of Congress.*"[199]

Assuming then that Congress has the authority to regulate the exercise of executive enforcement discretion, what limits exist, if any, to that authority?

There has been relatively little judicial discussion of the scope of Congress's authority to restrict the executive exercise of enforcement discretion. It is clear, however, that the judicial branch's reluctance to review executive branch prosecutorial and administrative enforcement decisions is grounded in a respect for the roles and functions of each branch of government; an acknowledgement that it would generally be improper and impractical for the court to review discretionary enforcement decisions made by executive branch officers; and the Take Care Clause, as control over the enforcement of law has been viewed as within the "special province of the Executive Branch" and an aspect of executive power that "lies at the core of the Executive's duty to see to the faithful execution of the laws."[200]

However, the presumption against the review of enforcement decisions is also founded upon statutory principles, limitations on judicial review imposed by the APA, and the notion that when Congress delegates enforcement authority to the executive branch, it intends to provide the agency with the discretion that traditionally accompanies those delegations. To the extent that judicial deference to executive enforcement decisions is based on statutory principles, it would appear that Congress must be free to modify the statutory environment and alter the traditional scope of enforcement discretion. Other forms of administrative discretion, for instance, can be enlarged, reduced, or altered by Congress through statute.[201]

While acknowledging that Congress can guide enforcement discretion, the Supreme Court has never directly addressed the precise limits of Congress's power, nor whether Congress can remove that discretion entirely by enacting mandatory enforcement language. Nor has the Court addressed whether Congress's authority to restrict administrative enforcement discretion differs in any meaningful way from its authority to restrict criminal prosecutorial discretion. A comparison of the strong constitutionally-based language used in cases addressing the executive's discretionary authority to initiate a criminal prosecution, with the mainly statutorily-based language in *Heckler*, would appear to suggest that Congress would have wider latitude in controlling civil or administrative enforcement actions than it would over federal criminal prosecutions. Justice Marshall, for instance, felt compelled to draw a distinction between prosecutorial and administrative discretion in his concurrence in *Heckler*, noting that it was "inappropriate to rely on notions of prosecutorial discretion to hold agency action unreviewable" because "arguments about prosecutorial discretion do not necessarily translate into the context of agency refusals to act."[202]

The Fifth Circuit has made a similar distinction based expressly on presidential power. In *Riley v. St. Luke's Episcopal Hospital*, the circuit court found intrusions into the executive's control over criminal cases to be more worrisome than intrusions into civil litigation.[203] The *Riley* court made this distinction in upholding the qui tam provision of the False Claims Act against a claim that the law unconstitutionally infringed on the executive's civil enforcement power.[204] The circuit court held that "no function cuts more to the heart of the Executive's constitutional duty to take care that the laws are faithfully executed than criminal prosecution."[205] The conduct of civil litigation, on the other hand, involved "lesser uses of traditional executive power."[206] Given the separate status accorded presidential control over criminal and civil matters, the court determined that:

> the Executive must wield two different types of control in order to ensure that its constitutional duties under Article II are not impinged. Should the occasion arise, these two different types of control necessarily require the application of two different sorts of tests.[207]

While it would appear that Congress may have greater authority over administrative enforcement discretion, legislation that can be characterized as significantly restricting the exercise of executive branch enforcement decisions, in either the criminal, civil, or administrative context, could raise questions under the separation of powers. This is especially true considering the Supreme Court has had little opportunity to address the precise contours and outer reaches of Congress's authority to impinge on discretionary executive enforcement decisions. In the absence of clearly established judicial precedent, the executive branch has historically opposed any judicial or legislative "interference" with enforcement decisions as a violation of the Take Care Clause.[208]

It may be helpful to first outline what would appear to be general limits to Congress's authority to intrude upon the executive's enforcement power. First, Congress may neither itself, nor through its officers, directly enforce federal law.[209] To exercise both the power to make and enforce the law would be an apparent violation of the separation of powers. The Supreme Court has clearly stated that "Legislative power, as distinguished from executive power, is the authority to make laws, but not to enforce them..."[210] James Madison outlined this fundamental principle in Federalist 47, where he characterized the accumulation of legislative and executive power in a single entity as "the very definition of tyranny."[211]

Second, Congress may neither appoint, nor reserve for itself the power to remove officers engaged in the enforcement of law. The Supreme Court's appointment and removal jurisprudence makes clear that Congress's role in selecting or controlling those who execute and enforce the law is severely limited.[212] The President, and the President alone, must be permitted a degree of control over those engaged in enforcement.[213] Congress may place limits on that control, by providing such officers with "for cause" removal restrictions, but it may not remove presidential control entirely.[214]

Third, it would appear unlikely that Congress could direct the executive to bring a criminal prosecution against a specific individual. In light of the Supreme Court's statement in *U.S. v. Nixon* that "the Executive Branch has exclusive authority and absolute discretion to decide whether to prosecute a case," the initiation of criminal prosecutions has been considered to be within the "special province of the executive branch" and at the heart of prosecutorial discretion.[215] The executive branch would presumably consider such a directive from Congress to be a significant intrusion into Presidential power.[216] Regardless of the validity of that position, there are other reasons why such legislation would be problematic. First, legislation that targets an individual for punishment may run afoul of the constitutional prohibition on bills of attainder.[217] Second, if Congress were to enact such a law, and the executive failed to comply, it is unlikely that a court would be willing to enforce the provision by issuing an order directing the executive branch to initiate a prosecution against a specific individual.[218]

Whether the separation of powers would be violated if Congress used less restrictive means to influence or confine the exercise of enforcement discretion, rather than to use its own officers to enforce the law or compel specific enforcement actions remains less clear. Any such legislation would presumably be evaluated under the standards established by the Supreme Court in *Morrison v. Olson*.[219] *Morrison*, as previously mentioned, involved a constitutional challenge to the independent counsel provisions of the Ethics in Government Act (EGA).[220] The EGA authorized the appointment of an independent counsel to investigate and prosecute high ranking executive branch officials for violations of certain federal laws. Under the statute, the Attorney General was required to conduct a preliminary investigation once he received "specific" and "credible" information alleging that certain executive officials had committed serious federal offenses.[221]

Under the now expired law, if the Attorney General determined that there were "reasonable grounds to believe that further investigation or prosecution [was] warranted" then the law stated that he "shall apply" to a special three-judge panel of the D.C. Circuit for the appointment of an independent counsel.[222] Once appointed, the independent counsel was granted "full power and independent authority to exercise all investigative and prosecutorial functions and powers of the [DOJ]" and was removable by the Attorney General "only for good cause."[223]

Former Assistant Attorney General Theodore Olson argued that by providing an individual, who was not under the President's control, with the authority to initiate and conduct criminal prosecutions, the law constituted an unconstitutional congressional intrusion into the President's enforcement power.[224] The court rejected this argument, determining that the law was consistent with the appointments clause; did not impermissibly expand the judicial function; did not infringe upon the President's removal power; and finally did not violate the separation of powers.[225]

With respect to the separation of powers, the Court determined that the law neither "'impermissibly undermine[s]' the powers of the Executive Branch, [n]or 'disrupts the proper balance between the coordinate branches [by] prevent[ing] the Executive Branch from accomplishing its constitutionally assigned functions.'"[226] In reaching this conclusion, the Court placed great weight on the fact that the independent counsel provisions did not "involve an attempt by Congress to increase its own powers at the expense of the Executive Branch."[227] Congress retained no powers of "control of supervision." Rather its role was limited to receiving reports and exercising oversight. Although the law clearly "reduce[d] the amount of control or supervision" exercised by the President over the "investigation and prosecution of a certain class of alleged criminal activity," it did not do so in an impermissible manner.[228] Furthermore, the President retained an adequate "degree of control over the power to initiate an investigation" because the Independent Counsel could be appointed only at the request of the Attorney General, and—"most importantly"—the Attorney General retained the power to remove the counsel for "good cause."[229] As a result, the court concluded:

> Notwithstanding the fact that the counsel is to some degree 'independent' and free from executive supervision to a greater extent than other federal prosecutors, in our view these features of the Act give the Executive Branch sufficient control over the independent counsel to ensure that the President is able to perform his constitutionally assigned duties.[230]

Justice Scalia's dissent in *Morrison* adopted a much stronger view of executive enforcement powers, holding that the investigation and prosecution of crimes was a "quintessential" and "exclusive" executive function.[231] Scalia would have invalidated the independent counsel provisions, and expressly rejected the majority's conclusion that "the ability to control the decision whether to investigate and prosecute the President's closest advisers, and indeed the President himself, is not 'so central to the functioning of the Executive Branch' as to be constitutionally required to be within the President's control."[232] He went on to assert that:

> We should say here that the President's constitutionally assigned duties include *complete* control over investigation and prosecution of violations of the law, and that the inexorable command of Article II is

clear and definite: the executive power must be vested in the President of the United States.[233]

Morrison may reasonably be interpreted as rejecting the notion that the executive's power over the enforcement of law is the type of core, or exclusive presidential power that is beyond the reach of Congress. The Court explicitly acknowledged, that it was "undeniable that the Act reduces the amount of control or supervision that the Attorney General and, through him, the President exercises over the investigation and prosecution of a certain class of alleged criminal activity."[234] That reduction, however, was not in itself unconstitutional. The majority opinion would appear to authorize legislative restrictions on the exercise of executive branch enforcement discretion, so long as Congress does not violate the established limitations previously discussed or otherwise "prevent the executive branch from accomplishing its constitutionally assigned functions."[235]

The Morrison standard for evaluating intrusions into the executive's enforcement power has been applied by a number of appellate courts in upholding the qui tam provision of the False Claims Act (FCA).[236] This provision authorizes a private person, known as the relator, to initiate a civil proceeding "in the name of the government" for violations of the FCA.[237] Upon filing a qui tam action, the relator must give notice to the government disclosing all material evidence the relator has gathered.[238] The government then has 60 days to investigate the allegations and determine whether it wishes to take control of the enforcement action or allow the relator to continue to "conduct" the proceeding.[239] If the government chooses to assume responsibility for the enforcement action, the relator may continue as a party, but the DOJ may make enforcement decisions without the approval of the relator, including a decision to dismiss the case or settle the claim.[240]

In a series of appellate level cases, the government argued that by granting private parties the authority to initiate a civil action on behalf of the United States, the FCA had violated the separation of powers and unconstitutionally infringed upon the President's enforcement function. Each circuit to review the question ultimately rejected this position, holding generally that the FCA does not impermissibly "interfere" with the President's constitutional functions under the Take Care Clause.[241] In applying the *Morrison* standard, the courts generally focused on the degree of control that the executive branch exercises over the relator, including the government's authority to intervene, place limits on the relators participation, restrict the relators power in discovery, and ultimately to decide whether to settle or dismiss the case. As such, although the provision may "*diminish* Executive branch control over the initiation and prosecution of a defined class of civil ligation," the Executive retains "'sufficient control' over the relator's conduct to insure that the President is able to perform his constitutionally assigned duty."[242]

Legislative Options to Deter Nonenforcement

Acknowledging the limitations imposed by the separation of powers, the precise scope of Congress's authority to counter agency policies of nonenforcement remains an open question. There may, however, be a number of ways in which Congress can use its legislative powers to encourage the executive branch to enforce laws in a manner reflective of Congress's will. [243] For example, it would appear that Congress may prohibit or require the consideration of certain factors in the decision to initiate an enforcement action, or affirmatively set enforcement priorities reflective of Congress's intent. With respect to permissible factors for consideration, the Court has made clear, in other contexts, that it will reject agency action where the agency has "relied on factors which Congress has not intended it to consider."[244] With respect to setting enforcement priorities, the Supreme Court acknowledged in *Heckler* that congress may set "substantive priorities" for an agency to follow in exercising its enforcement power.[245] Further support for Congress's prominent role in setting agency priorities appears in *TVA v. Hill.*[246] There, the Court stated "emphatically" that it is "the exclusive province of the Congress not only to formulate legislative policies and mandate programs and projects, but also to establish their relative priority for the Nation. Once Congress [] has decided the order of priorities in a given area, it is for the Executive to administer the laws and for the courts to enforce them when enforcement is sought."[247] If Congress does utilize its legislative authority to set enforcement priorities or establish factors for consideration in making enforcement decisions, it would appear to be within the judicial authority to ensure executive compliance with those explicit statutory requirements. This would especially be the case in a situation where a stated agency enforcement policy is in direct conflict with the statutory framework.

Whether Congress can *remove* the discretion to initiate an enforcement action by establishing a generally applicable statutory framework that *requires* the executive branch to enforce the law, not against specific individuals, but rather under certain factual scenarios; where certain criteria are met; or where certain aggravating factors are present; may raise concerns. This is especially true in the criminal context, where some courts have made broad statements about the nature of the executive's power to decide whether to bring a criminal prosecution.[248] But these statements have generally occurred in opinions that either focus the power of the *courts* (as opposed to Congress) to interfere in prosecutorial decisions, or that avoid the question of congressional authority by interpreting a statute as insufficient to curtail prosecutorial discretion.[249] Although no court appears to have directly addressed the issue, the Supreme Court did note in *U.S. v. Nixon* that "the Executive Branch has *exclusive* authority and *absolute discretion* to decide whether to prosecute a case."[250] While the value of the *Nixon* dicta is debatable,[251] it nevertheless suggests that congressional attempts to require prosecutions may be problematic.[252]

The executive branch has previously determined that Congress lacks the authority to compel prosecutions in the criminal context. In its evaluation of whether the criminal contempt statute[253] requires the U.S. Attorney to refer a contempt citation to the grand jury, the DOJ argued that "although prosecutorial discretion may be regulated to a certain extent by Congress and in some instances by the Constitution, *the decision not to prosecute* an individual may not be controlled because it is fundamental to the executive's prerogative."[254] The DOJ went on to assert that "divesting" a federal prosecutor of the discretion to decide whether to bring a prosecution would "run afoul...of the separation of powers by stripping the Executive of its proper constitutional authority and by vesting improper power in Congress."[255]

The DOJ position was reached four years prior to the Supreme Court's important decision on Presidential control over the enforcement of law in *Morrison*. Under *Morrison*, the standard for evaluating the separation of powers concerns associated with a law that arguably intrudes on the President's personal obligation to "take Care that the laws be faithfully executed" would appear to be whether the law "'impermissibly undermine[s]' the powers of the Executive Branch," or "prevent[s] the Executive Branch from accomplishing its constitutionally assigned functions."[256]

The chief considerations in the *Morrison* analysis appear to have related to "aggrandizement" and "control." The Court upheld the independent counsel provisions because Congress had not sought to aggrandize its own powers (the independent counsel was "independent" from both the President and Congress), and because the President, through the Attorney General, retained sufficient "supervision" and "control" over actions of the independent counsel.[257] How a court would apply these principles to a law that sought to compel a criminal prosecution upon the occurrence of certain conditions is difficult to determine. It could be argued that by mandating scenarios under which criminal prosecutions must occur, Congress is, in effect, replacing the prosecutor's discretionary decision of whether to initiate a case, with its own congressional determination. This could be seen as "controlling" the exercise of a discretionary enforcement decision, depriving the President of adequate control over federal prosecutors, and an "aggrandizement" of congressional power, as Congress would have vested power in *itself* to determine when and whether prosecutions are to be initiated. [258] To the contrary, a court may be equally likely to decide that such a law is a permissible legislative restriction on the exercise of the initial discretionary decision of whether to initiate a prosecution that neither aggrandizes Congress's power nor subverts Presidential control, as the conduct of the prosecution, once initiated, remains entirely in the hands of the executive branch. Characterized in this manner, Congress has acted to limit, but not remove, executive control over enforcement. *Morrison* and the qui tam cases suggest that it is constitutionally permissible for Congress to "reduce" or "diminish" executive branch control over the initiation of an enforcement action.[259] In addition, constitutional issues may be ameliorated by ensuring that the executive branch retains significant discretion to determine whether the conditions that trigger the mandated prosecution are met.[260]

In the administrative context, *Heckler's* approval of the reasoning in *Dunlop* would appear to approve of legislation that creates a mandatory administrative enforcement framework.[261] Even so, obtaining a court order actually compelling enforcement may be difficult, as was evident in how the *Dunlop* case ultimately concluded. As previously discussed, the Supreme Court stated that the "principle of absolute prosecutorial discretion" was inapplicable in *Dunlop* because Congress had, by statute, required the Secretary to bring an enforcement action if certain "clearly defined" factors were present.[262] In confirming the continued validity of *Dunlop*, the Court in *Heckler* stated that "The statute being administered quite clearly withdrew discretion from the agency and provided guidelines for exercise of its enforcement power."[263] The removal of discretion, the Court held, was a:

> decision [] in the first instance for Congress... If it has indicated an intent to circumscribe agency enforcement discretion, and has provided meaningful standards for defining the limits of that discretion, there is 'law to apply' under [the APA] and courts may require that the agency follow that law; if it has not, then an agency refusal to institute proceedings is a decision 'committed to agency discretion by law.'[264]

However, the court did not order the Secretary to initiate an enforcement proceeding, but rather directed the Secretary to file a "statement of reasons" as to why no action was brought and directed the district court to review that document to determine whether the nonenforcement decision was "arbitrary and capricious."[265] The court further directed that if the district court "determines that the Secretary's statement of reasons adequately demonstrates that his decision not to sue is not contrary to law, the ... suit fails and should be dismissed."[266] The court then noted that if the district court came to the opposite conclusion, new concerns under the separation of powers may arise, stating:

> The district court may, however, ultimately come to the conclusion that the Secretary's statement of reasons on its face renders necessary the conclusion that his decision not to sue is so irrational as to constitute the decision arbitrary and capricious. There would then be presented the question whether the district court is empowered to order the Secretary to bring a civil suit against the union to set aside the election. We have no occasion to address that question at this time. It obviously presents some difficulty in light of the strong evidence that Congress deliberately gave exclusive enforcement authority to the Secretary. We prefer therefore at this time to assume that the Secretary would proceed appropriately without the coercion of a court order when finally advised by the courts that his decision was in law arbitrary and capricious.[267]

In a footnote, the Court noted the union's argument that the separation of powers does not "countenance a court order requiring the executive branch, against its wishes, to institute a lawsuit in federal court."[268] The Court stated only that "[s]ince we do not consider at this time the question of the court's power to order the Secretary to file suit, we need not address [the separation of powers] contentions."[269] On remand, the district court found the provided statement of reasons to be inadequate to justify the agency inaction, but again, did not order the Secretary to initiate an enforcement action. Instead it simply directed a reconsideration of the agency decision and prohibited the Secretary from using a method of determining whether a violation occurred that the court found to be inconsistent with congressional intent.[270]

End Notes

[1] The Obama Administration is not the first Presidential Administration to use nonenforcement as a means of achieving policy goals. See, e.g., Zachary S. Price, Enforcement Discretion and Executive Duty, 67 Vand. L. Rev. 671, 686 (2014) ("The George W. Bush Administration apparently underenforced certain environmental, product safety, and civil rights laws as a matter of policy; in one case the Environmental Protection Agency stopped enforcing certain air pollution restrictions after the D.C. Circuit declared its regulatory standards too permissive. Critics also accused the Clinton and Bush Administrations of neglecting enforcement of gun safety laws, and the Reagan Administration of deliberately failing to enforce antitrust statutes.")(citations omitted).

[2] These decisions should be distinguished from the Obama Administration's decision not to prosecute Attorney General Eric Holder for criminal contempt of Congress. The executive branch policy of not enforcing the criminal contempt statute against an executive branch official asserting executive privilege in response to a congressional subpoena— which dates at least to the Reagan Administration—is based on constitutional objections. See e.g., U.S. v. Windsor, 133 S. Ct. 2675, 2702 (2013) (Scalia, J. dissenting) ("This suit saw the light of day only because the President enforced the Act (and thus gave Windsor standing to sue) even though he believed it unconstitutional. He could have equally chosen (more appropriately, some would say) neither to enforce nor to defend the statute he believed to be unconstitutional...").

[3] See, CRS Report R43034, State Legalization of Recreational Marijuana: Selected Legal Issues, by Todd Garvey and Brian T. Yeh.

[4] Memorandum for selected U.S. Attorneys from David W. Ogden, Deputy Attorney General, Investigations and Prosecutions in States Authorizing the Medical Use of Marijuana, October 19, 2009, available at http://www.justice.gov/opa/documents/medical-marijuana.pdf.

[5] Memorandum for U.S. Attorneys from James M. Cole, Deputy Attorney General, Guidance Regarding Marijuana Enforcement, August 29, 2013, available at http://www.justice.gov/iso/opa/resources/3052013829132756857467.pdf.

[6] Janet Napolitano, Secretary of Homeland Security, Exercising Prosecutorial Discretion with Respect to Individuals Who Came to the United States as Children, June 15, 2012, at 1, available at http://www.dhs.gov/xlibrary/assets/s1- exercising-prosecutorial-discretion-individuals-who-came-to-us-as-children.pdf.

[7] The Memorandum lays out the precise criteria to be satisfied "before an individual is considered for an exercise of prosecutorial discretion":

- came to the United States under the age of sixteen;
- has continuously resided in the United states for at least five years preceding the date of this memorandum and is present in the United states on the date of this memorandum;
- is currently in school, has graduated from high school, has obtained a general education development certificate, or is an honorably discharged veteran of the Coast Guard or Armed Forces of the United States;
- has not been convicted of a felony offense, a significant misdemeanor offense, multiple misdemeanor offenses, or otherwise poses a threat to national security or public safety; and
- is not above the age of thirty.

Id. See also, CRS Report R42924, Prosecutorial Discretion in Immigration Enforcement: Legal Issues, by Kate M. Manuel and Todd Garvey.

[8] See, Crane v. Napolitano, 920 F. Supp. 2d 724 (N.D. Tex. 2013).

[9] See, CRS Legal Sidebar, Obama Administration Delays Implementation of ACA's Employer Responsibility Requirements: A Brief Legal Overview.

[10] 79 Fed. Reg. 8544 (Feb. 12 2014).

[11] See, Letter from Gary Cohen, Director, Center for Consumer Information and Insurance Oversight, Centers for Medicare and Medicaid Services, to State Insurance Commissioners (Nov. 14, 2013) available at: http://www.cms.gov/CCIIO/Resources/Letters/Downloads/commissioner-letter-11-14-2013.PDF; CRS Legal Sidebar, Obama Administration's "Fix" for Insurance Cancellations: A Legal Overview.

[12] See, e.g., H.Rept. 113-376 113th Cong. (2014); H.Rept. 113-377 113th Cong. (2014).

[13] H.R. 3973, Faithful Execution of the Law Act, 113th Cong. (2014).

[14] H.R. 4138 113th Cong. (2014).

[15] H. Res. 676 113th Cong. (2014).

[16] See, e.g., Medellin v. Texas, 552 U.S. 491, 532 (U.S. 2008) ("This authority allows the President to execute the laws, not make them."); Youngstown Sheet & Tube Co. v. Sawyer, 343 U.S. 579, 587 (1952) ("[T]he President's power to see that the laws are faithfully executed refutes the idea that he is to be a lawmaker. The Constitution limits his functions in the lawmaking process to the recommending of laws he thinks wise and the vetoing of laws he thinks bad."); Myers v. United States, 272 U.S. 52, 177(1926) ("The duty of the President to see that the laws be executed is a duty that does not go beyond the laws or require him to achieve more than Congress sees fit to leave within his power."); Lear Siegler, Inc. v. Lehman, 842 F. 2d 1102, 1124 (9th Cir. 1988) ("To construe this duty to faithfully execute the laws as implying the power to forbid their execution perverts the clear language of the 'take care' clause. ."), reh'g en banc ordered sub nom. Lear Seigler, Inc. v. Ball, 863 F. 2d 693 (9th Cir. 1988) (en banc); National Treasury Employees Union v. Nixon, 492 F. 2d 587, 604 (D.C.Cir. 1974) ("That constitutional duty does not permit the President to refrain from executing laws duly enacted by the Congress as those laws are construed by the judiciary.").

[17] See, e.g., Free Enter. Fund v. Pub. Co. Accounting Oversight Bd., 561 U.S. 477 (2010) ("The President cannot 'take Care that the Laws be faithfully executed' if he cannot oversee the faithfulness of the officers who execute them."); Buckley v. Valeo, 424 U.S. 1 (1976) ("A lawsuit is the ultimate remedy for a breach of the law, and it is to the President, and not to the Congress, that the Constitution entrusts the responsibility to 'take Care that the Laws be faithfully executed.'"); U.S. v. Nixon, 418 U.S. 683, 693 (1974)("the Executive Branch has exclusive authority and absolute discretion to decide whether to prosecute a case"); U.S. v. Armstrong, 517 U.S. 456, 464 (1996) ("They have this latitude because they are designated by statute as the President's delegates to help him discharge his constitutional responsibility to 'take Care that the Laws be faithfully executed.'"); Confiscation Cases, 74 U.S. 454 (1869); Smith v. U.S., 375 F.2d 243 (5th Cir. 1967) ("The President of the United States is charged in Article 2, Section 3, of the Constitution with the duty to 'take Care that the Laws be faithfully executed'...The discretion...in choosing whether to prosecute or not to prosecute, or to abandon a prosecution already started, is absolute."); U.S. v. Cox, 342 F.2d 167 (5th Cir. 1965)("It follows, as an incident of the constitutional separation of powers, that the courts are not to interfere with the free exercise of the discretionary powers of the attorneys of the United States in their control over criminal prosecutions.").

[18] U.S. Const. Art. II, §3 ("He shall from time to time give to the Congress Information on the State of the Union, and recommend to their Consideration such Measures as he shall judge necessary and expedient...").

[19] U.S. Const. Art. I, §7 ("Every Bill which shall have passed the House of Representatives and the Senate, shall, before it become a Law, be presented to the President of the United States; If he approves he shall sign it, but if not he shall return it, with his Objections to that House in which it shall have originated...").

[20] U.S. Const. Art. II, §1 ("The executive Power shall be vested in a President of the United States of America.").

[21] One way in which the President communicates his views on bills currently under consideration is through Statements of Administration Policy. See, http://www.whitehouse. gov/omb/ legislative_sap_default.

[22] Youngstown Sheet & Tube Co. v. Sawyer, 343 U.S. 579 (1952) ("The Constitution limits his functions in the lawmaking process to the recommending of laws he thinks wise and the vetoing of laws he thinks bad.")

[23] The President's obligation to execute the law is equally applicable whether the law was enacted with the approval of the President or by a congressional override of the President's veto.

[24] U.S. Const. Art. II, §3 ("[H]e shall take Care that the Laws be faithfully executed.")

[25] See, e.g., Zachary S. Price, Enforcement Discretion and Executive Duty, 67 Vand. L. Rev. 671, 693 (2014). Beyond this limited agreement, there is little consensus among scholars as to the historical meaning of the Take Care Clause. Compare Steven G. Calabresi and Saikrishna B. Prakash, The President's Power to Execute the Laws, 104 Yale L. J. 541 (1994) with Lawrence Lessig and Cass R. Sunstein, The President and the Administration, 94 Colum. L. Rev. 1 (1994).

[26] 2 James Wilson, Lectures on Law Part 2, in Collected Works of James Wilson 829, 878 (2007).

[27] Memorandum from Walter Dellinger, Assistant Attorney General, Office of Legal Counsel, Re: Consitutional Limitations on Federal Government Participation in Binding Arbitration (Sept. 7 1995).

[28] See, INS v. Chadha, 462 U.S. 919, 945 (1983) ("Explicit and unambiguous provisions of the Constitution prescribe and define the respective functions of the Congress and of the Executive in the legislative process.").

[29] See, Clinton v. City of New York, 524 U.S. 417, 488 (1998) ("There is no provision in the Constitution that authorizes the President to enact, to amend, or to repeal statutes.").

[30] Kendall v. United States ex. rel. Stokes, 37 U.S. (12 Pet.) 524, 613 (1838).

[31] 5 U.S. 137 (1803).

[32] Id. at 166.

[33] Id. at 164 ("Is the act of delivering or withholding a commission to be considered as a mere political act, belonging to the executive department alone, for the performance of which entire confidence is placed by our constitution in the supreme executive; and for any misconduct respecting which, the injured individual has no remedy?").

[34] 37 U.S. 524 (1838).

[35] Id. at 610.

[36] Id.

[37] Id. at 613.

[38] Id.

[39] Id.

[40] 343 U.S. 579 (1952).

[41] Id. at 587-88. ("[T]he Constitution limits his functions in the lawmaking process to the recommending of laws he thinks wise and the vetoing of laws he thinks bad. And the Constitution is neither silent nor equivocal about who shall make laws which the President is to execute.").

[42] Id. at 587.

[43] Id. at 655 (Jackson, J. concurring).

[44] See, Clinton v. City of New York, 524 U.S. 417, 468 (1998) (Kennedy, J. concurring)("President Nixon, the Mahatma Gandhi of all impounders, asserted at a press conference in 1973 that his 'constitutional right' to impound appropriated funds was 'absolutely clear.'").

[45] See, e.g., State Highway Comm'n. of Missouri v. Volpe, 479 F.2d 1099 (8th Cir. 1973); Pennsylvania v. Lynn, 501 F.2d 848 (D.C. Cir. 1974); Local 2677, American Fed. of Gov. Employees v. Phillips, 358 F. Supp. 60 (D.D.C. 1973).

[46] 420 U.S. 35 (1975). Lower federal courts similarly rejected President Reagan's assertion that he had the authority to disregard the automatic stay provisions of the Competition in Contracting Act (CICA). President Reagan objected to the law on constitutional grounds, asserting that the law frustrated the separation of powers by delegating executive powers to a legislative branch officer in violation of the principles established in INS v. Chadha, 462 U.S. 919 (1983) and Bowsher v. Synar, 478 US. 714 (1986). Consistent with the President's view, the Office of Management and Budget issued a directive to all executive branch agencies to disregard the stay provisions of the law. An initial decision in Lear Siegler, Inc. v. Lehman, 842 F.2d 1102 (9th Cir. 1988) by the U.S. Court of Appeals for the Ninth Circuit (Ninth Circuit) held that CICA did not impermissibly intrude on the President's authority to execute the laws, but also contained strong language criticizing the President's nonenforcement decision. The government asserted that nonenforcement was warranted "because the President's duty to uphold the Constitution and faithfully execute the laws empowers the President to interpret the Constitution and disregard laws he deems unconstitutional." Id. at 1121. The court rejected this argument, holding the position to be "utterly at odds with the texture and plain language of the Constitution, and with nearly two centuries of judicial precedent." Id. In an approach slightly different from that taken by other courts, the Ninth Circuit reasoned that the President's asserted power would provide the President with "absolute veto power" by vitiating Congress's constitutional authority to override a Presidential veto. Id. at 1124. By unilaterally suspending a law, as opposed to vetoing the law, the President "afforded no opportunity for congressional override, thereby violating the override as well as the veto provision of the Constitution." Id. On appeal en banc, however, the Ninth Circuit withdrew the above quoted portions on other grounds. Lear Siegler v. Lehman, 893 F.2d 205 (9th Cir. 1989) ("Accordingly, Part III of the decision...is withdrawn from publication...").

[47] Local 2677, American Fed. of Gov. Employees v. Phillips, 358 F. Supp. 60, 76 (D.D.C. 1973); Lincoln v. Vigil, 508 U.S. 182, 193 (1993) ("Of course, an agency is not free simply to disregard statutory responsibilities: Congress may always circumscribe agency discretion to allocate resources by putting restrictions in the operative statutes...").

[48] Id. at 77.

[49] See, e.g., Ameron Inc. v. U.S. Army Corps of Engineers, 808 F.2d 979, 993 (3rd Cir. 1986) ("If Congress gives the President only a few general instructions, and allows the executive 'to fill up the details,' then the scope of the executive power is great. If, on the other hand, Congress chooses to specify a great number of details concerning how it wants the

executive to proceed, such as specifying what it wants the executive to procure, the legislature is entirely free to take that course.") (citations omitted).

[50] Wilbur v. United States ex rel. Kadrie, 281 U.S. 206, 219 (1930) ("Where the duty . . . depends upon a statute or statutes the construction or application of which is not free from doubt, it is regarded as involving the character of judgment or discretion which cannot be controlled by mandamus.").

[51] Ameron, 808 F.2d at 994.

[52] See, Free Enter. Fund v. PCAOB, 130 S. Ct. 3138, 3151 (2010) ("As Madison stated on the floor of the First Congress, 'if any power whatsoever is in its nature Executive, it is the power of appointing, overseeing, and controlling those who execute the laws.' 1 Annals of Cong. 463 (1789).").

[53] See, e.g., Id. at 3152 ("Article II confers on the President 'the general administrative control of those executing the laws.' It is his responsibility to take care that the laws be faithfully executed. The buck stops with the President, in Harry Truman's famous phrase.")(citations omitted); Nixon v. Fitzgerald, 457 U.S. 731, 750, (1982) ("This grant of authority establishes the President as the chief constitutional officer of the Executive Branch, entrusted with supervisory and policy responsibilities of utmost discretion and sensitivity. These include the enforcement of federal law—it is the President who is charged constitutionally to 'take Care that the Laws be faithfully executed'").

[54] 478 U.S. 714 (1986).

[55] Id. at 723.

[56] 424 U.S. 1 (1976).

[57] Id. at 138.

[58] 521 U.S. 898 (1997).

[59] Id. at 922 (citations omitted).

[60] Free Enter. Fund v. Pub. Co. Accounting Oversight Bd., 561 U.S. 477 (2010).

[61] Id. at 3147, 3152.

[62] 487 U.S. 654, 690 (1988).

[63] Id. at 693.

[64] U.S. v. Armstrong, 517 U.S. at 464 ("They have this latitude because they are designated by statute as the President's delegates to help him discharge his constitutional responsibility to 'take Care that the Laws be faithfully executed.'");

[65] Wayte v. U.S., 470 U.S. 598, 607 (1985) ("In our criminal justice system, the Government retains 'broad discretion' as to whom to prosecute.")(citing United States v. Goodwin, 457 U.S. 368, 380 (1982)); United States v. Nixon, 418 U.S. 683, 693 (1974) ("[T]he Executive Branch has exclusive authority and absolute discretion to decide whether to prosecute a case...") (citing the Confiscation Cases, 74 U.S. 454 (1869)).

[66] See, e.g., Rebecca Krauss, The Theory of Prosecutorial Discretion in Federal Law: Origins and Development, 6 Seton Hall Cir. Rev. 1, 19-26 (2009) (describing the English use of the nolle prosequi and its "absorb[tion]" by American law).

[67] Id. at 20.

[68] See, e.g., Confiscation Cases, 74 U.S. 454 (1869); Newman v. United States, 382 F.2d 479, 480 (D.C. Cir. 1967) ("Most recently, the issue of the United States Attorney's 'discretionary control of criminal prosecutions has arisen in connection with the filing of a nolle prosequi, and the Courts have regularly refused to interfere with these voluntary dismissals of prosecution.'") (citing Louis B. Schwartz, Federal Criminal Jurisdiction and Prosecutors' Discretion, 13 Law & Contemp. Prob. 64, 83 (1948)).

[69] See, e.g., Armstrong, 517 U.S. at 464 ("They have this latitude because they are designated by statute as the President's delegates to help him discharge his constitutional responsibility to 'take Care that the Laws be faithfully executed.'"); Confiscation Cases, 74 U.S. at 458 ("Appointed, as the Attorney General is, in pursuance of an act of Congress, to prosecute and conduct such suits, argument would seem to be unnecessary to prove his authority to dispose of these cases in the manner proposed.... "); Ponzi v. Fessenden, 258 U.S. 254, 262 (1922) ("The Attorney General is the head of the Department of Justice. He is the hand of the President in taking care that the laws of the United States in protection of the interests of the United States in legal proceedings and in the prosecution of offences be faithfully executed."); Smith v. Meese, 821 F.2d 1484, 1491 (11th Cir. 1987) ("The prosecutorial function, and the discretion that accompanies it, is thus committed by the Constitution to the executive, and the judicial branch's deference to the executive on prosecutorial decisionmaking is grounded in the constitutional separation of powers."); United States v. Cox, 342 F.2d 167, 171 (5th Cir. 1965) ("as an incident of the constitutional separation of powers...the courts are not to interfere with the free exercise of the discretionary powers of the attorneys of the United States in their control over criminal prosecutions.").

[70] Smith v. Meese, 821 F.2d 1484, 1491 (11th Cir. 1987).

[71] Wayte v. U.S., 470 U.S. 598, 607 (1985).

[72] Id. at 607-608 ("Such factors as the strength of the case, the prosecution's general deterrence value, the Government's enforcement priorities, and the case's relationship to the Government's overall enforcement plan are not readily susceptible to the kind of analysis the courts are competent to undertake. Judicial supervision in this area, moreover, entails systemic costs of particular concern. Examining the basis of a prosecution delays the criminal proceeding, threatens to chill law enforcement by subjecting the prosecutor's motives and decisionmaking to outside inquiry, and may undermine prosecutorial effectiveness by revealing the Government's enforcement policy. All these are substantial concerns that make the courts properly hesitant to examine the decision whether to prosecute.").

[73] Newman v. U.S., 382 F.2d 479, 480 (D.C. Cir. 1967).

[74] See, e.g., Heckler v Chaney, 470 U.S. 821, 832 (1985) ("The decision of a prosecutor in the Executive Branch not to indict . . . has long been regarded as the special province of the Executive Branch, inasmuch as it is the Executive who is charged by the Constitution to 'take Care that the Laws be faithfully executed.'");

[75] 418 U.S. 683, 693 (1974).

[76] 342 F.2d 167 (5th Cir. 1965).

[77] Id. at 171.

[78] 477 F. 2d 375 (2nd Cir. 1973).

[79] Id. at 381.

[80] Id. at 379.

[81] Id. at 380.

[82] See, Prosecution for Contempt of Congress of an Executive Branch Official Who Has Asserted a Claim of Executive Privilege, 8 Op. Off. Legal Counsel 101, 114 (1984) (emphasis added). This traditional conception may, however, have been qualified in some respects following the Supreme Court's decision in Morrison v. Olson, in which the Court upheld a congressional delegation of prosecutorial power to an independent counsel under the Ethics in Government Act. 487 U.S. 654 (1988).

[83] 8 Op. Off. Legal Counsel 101, 115 (1984).

[84] United States v. Batchelder, 442 U.S. 114, 125 (1979).

[85] Smith v. Meese, 821 F.2d 1484, 1492 (11th Cir. 1987).

[86] Bordenkircher v. Hayes, 434 U.S. 357, 364 (1977) (finding that a state prosecutor's decision to indict the defendant as habitual offender after he refused to plead guilty of a felony did not violate the defendant's constitutional rights).

[87] United States v. Goodwin, 457 U.S. 368, 372 (1982).

[88] U.S. v. Johnson, 577 F.2d 1304 (5th Cir. 1978)

[89] 118 U.S. 356 (1886).

[90] Reno v. American-Arab Anti-Discrimination Comm, 525 U.S. 471, 489 (1999) (quoting Armstrong, 517 U.S. at 463). Specifically, they must show that: (1) they were singled out for prosecution on an impermissible basis; (2) the government had a policy of declining to prosecute similarly situated defendants of other races, religions, etc.; and (3) the policy was motivated by a discriminatory purpose.

[91] 497 F.2d 676, 679 n.19 (1974).

[92] Id.

[93] NAACP v. Levi, 418 F. Supp. 1109, 1116 (D.D.C. 1976).

[94] 359 F.2d 234 (D.C. Cir. 1965).

[95] Id. at 235.

[96] See, 42 U.S.C. §§1984, 1986, 1987, 1988.

[97] Inmates of Attica Correctional Facility v. Rockefeller, 477 F.2d 375 (2nd Cir. 1973); Moses v. Kennedy, 219 F. Supp. 762 (D.D.C. 1963).

[98] Inmates of Attica Correctional Facility, 477 F.2d at 381.

[99] Id. at 382.

[100] In a concurring opinion in Nathan v. Smith, 737 F.2d 1069 (D.C. Cir. 1984) Judge Bork identified the "severity of the constitutional problem that would arise" were Congress to authorize the courts to direct the Attorney General in his law enforcement function.

[101] Heckler v. Chaney, 470 U.S. at 832 ("[W]e recognize that an agency's refusal to institute proceedings shares to some extent the characteristics of the decision of a prosecutor in the Executive Branch not to indict — a decision which has long been regarded as the special province of the Executive Branch, inasmuch as it is the Executive who is charged by the Constitution to 'take Care that the Laws be faithfully executed.'"). It would appear that agency enforcement discretion exercised in the administrative context, though similar, is to be distinguished from prosecutorial discretion exercised in the criminal context.

[102] 5 U.S.C. §701(a).

[103] Citizens to Preserve Overton Park, Inc. v. Volpe, 401 U.S. 402, 410 (1971) (holding that the "committed to agency discretion" exception to judicial review is "very narrow" and "is applicable in those rare instances where 'statutes are drawn in such broad terms that in a given case there is no law to apply.') (citing S. Rep. No. 752, 79th Cong., 1st Sess., 26 (1945)).

[104] It should be noted that the dismissal of a challenge to an agency nonenforcement decision under the APA is not necessarily recognition by the court that the agency was acting within its authority. A legal distinction must be made between a decision in which a court reviews the merits of a challenge and approves of the agency action or inaction, and one in which a court dismisses the challenge for lack of jurisdiction before reviewing the merits. Although, as a practical matter, either decision results in the same outcome, (i.e., the continuation of the agency decision) it would be inappropriate to state that a court that has dismissed a nonenforcement decision as "committed to agency discretion" has accorded legal confirmation to the agency action or inaction. See also, Johnson v. U.S. Office of Pers. Mgmt., No. 14-C-009, slip op. at 17 (E.D. Wisc. July 21, 2014) ("[T]here is nothing in the

Constitution stipulating that all wrongs must have remedies, much less that the remedy must lie in federal court.").

105 For a typical description of how agencies exercise enforcement discretion see, Securities and Exchange Commission Division of Enforcement: Enforcement Manual, 2.1.1 Ranking Investigations and Allocating Resources, available at: http://www.sec.gov/divisions/enforce/enforcementmanual.pdf.

106 5 U.S.C. §701(a).

107 470 U.S. 821.

108 Id. at 831.

109 Id.

110 Id. at 831-32.

111 Id. at 832.

112 One commentator has identified seven exceptions to the Heckler v. Chaney rule, concluding that it "would probably be a mistake to read Chaney as establishing a general rule of nonreviewabilty for enforcement decisions." See, Cass Sunstein, Reviewing Agency Inaction After Heckler v. Chaney, 52 U. Chi. L. Rev. 653, 675-683 (1985). These exceptions include: "Inaction Based on Constitutionally Impermissible Factors;" "Inaction Based on Asserted Absence of Statutory Jurisdiction;" "Inaction Based on Statutorily Irrelevant Factors or Otherwise in Violation of Statutory Constraints on Enforcement Discretion;" "'Abdication' of Statutory Duty or a 'Pattern' of Nonenforcement;" "Refusal to Enforce Agency Regulations;" "Failure to Initiate Rulemaking;" "Generalized Arbitrariness." The D.C Circuit has also held that the Heckler presumption does not apply when a nonenforcement decision is actually an agency interpretation of a statute. See, Edison Elec. Inst. v. EPA, 996 F.2d 326, 333 (D.C. Cir. 1993) ("'[N]othing in the holding or policy of Heckler v. Chaney [] precludes review of a ...challenge of an agency's announcement of its interpretation of a statute,' even when that interpretation is advanced in the context of a decision not to take enforcement action.") (citations omitted).

113 Heckler, at 833.

114 Id. at 833 n.4.

115 The dearth of case law relating to agency nonenforcement may be due to the difficulty of finding a plaintiff who has been sufficiently injured by the agency inaction, such that the individual can establish standing. See e.g., CRS Legal Sidebar, Obama Administration Delays Implementation of ACA's Employer Responsibility Requirements: A Brief Legal Overview. The U.S. District Court for the Southern District of Florida recently dismissed a challenge to the administration's delayed enforcement of the employer mandate for lack of standing. Kawa Orthodontics, LLP v. Lew, Case No. 13-80990-CIV-DIMITROULEAS (D. Fl. Jan. 13, 2014). Justice Scalia articulated his views of how the standing doctrine generally should bar challenges to executive nonenforcement decisions in his dissent in FEC v. Atkins, 524 U.S. 11 (1998)(Scalia, J. dissenting) ("The provision of law at issue in this case is an extraordinary one, conferring upon a private person the ability to bring an Executive agency into court to compel its enforcement of the law against a third party. Despite its liberality, the [APA] does not allow such suits, since enforcement action is traditionally deemed 'committed to agency discretion by law.' If provisions such as the present one were commonplace, the role of the Executive Branch in our system of separated and equilibrated powers would be greatly reduced, and that of the Judiciary greatly expanded.")(citations omitted).

116 Heckler, 470 U.S. at 833. See also, Souder v. Brennan, 367 F. Supp. 808, 811-12 (D.D.C. 1973) ("It is undisputed that the Department of Labor has a declared policy of

nonenforcement of the minimum wage and overtime provisions with regard to patient-workers at non-Federal institutions for the mentally-ill. It is also clear to the Court that if the Fair Labor Standards Act does apply to such patient-workers then the policy of nonenforcement is a violation of the Secretary's duty to enforce the law.").

[117] Id. at 834.

[118] Id. at 834-35.

[119] The D.C. Circuit has suggested that "guidelines" can take the form of "standards in the statute itself, in regulations promulgated by an administrative agency in carrying out its statutory mandate, or in other binding expressions of agency viewpoint." Crowley Caribbean Transp. v. Pena, 37 F.3d 671, 677 (D.C. Cir. 1994) (citations omitted).

[120] 21 U.S.C. §372.

[121] Heckler, 470 U.S. at 835.

[122] Id.

[123] Id. at 839 (Brennan, J. concurring.)

[124] Id.

[125] Id.

[126] 421 U.S. 560 (1975).

[127] 29 U.S.C. §482.

[128] Dunlop v. Bachowski, 421 U.S. 560, 567 n.7 (1975) ("We agree with the Court of Appeals, for the reasons stated in its opinion, 502 F. 2d 79, 86-88 (CA3 1974), that there is no merit in the Secretary's contention that his decision is an unreviewable exercise of prosecutorial discretion."); Bachowski v. Brennan, 502 F.2d 79, 87 (3rd Cir. 1974).

[129] Bachowski v. Brennan, 502 F.2d 79, 87 (3rd Cir. 1974).

[130] Id. at 88 (citing Davis, Administrative Law Treatise, §28.16 at 984 (1970 Supp.).

[131] Id.

[132] Id.

[133] Dunlop, at 571. ("Since the statute relies upon the special knowledge and discretion of the Secretary for the determination of both the probable violation and the probable effect, clearly the reviewing court is not authorized to substitute its judgment for the decision of the Secretary not to bring suit.").

[134] Heckler, 470 U.S. at 834.

[135] Id.

[136] Atlantic Green Sea Turtle v. County Council of Volusia County, 2005 U.S. Dist. LEXIS 38841 (May 3, 2005).

[137] Id. at 49.

[138] Id. Similarly, in Tucci v. District of Columbia, a Washington D.C. court considered whether a D.C. law providing that "the Mayor of the District of Columbia...shall enforce the District of Columbia Solid Waste Management and Multi-Material Recycling Act of 1988," removed the Mayor's enforcement discretion. The court analogized the provision to the common use of the phrase "shall be prosecuted," holding that:

No one would seriously argue that the use of the term "shall be prosecuted" in these statutes requires the...United States Attorney to prosecute each and every violation of these statutes brought to his or her attention. Similarly here, the words "the Mayor ... shall enforce" allocate responsibility — they do not strip the Mayor of discretion in undertaking enforcement action. 956 A. 2d 684 (2008).

[139] Crane v. Napolitano, 2013 U.S. Dist. LEXIS 57788 (N.D. TX, April 23, 2013); Janet Napolitano, Secretary of Homeland Security, Exercising Prosecutorial Discretion with Respect to Individuals Who Came to the United States as Children, June 15, 2012, at 1.

[140] Crane, at 7-13.

[141] 8 U.S.C. §1225.

[142] Crane, at 39 ("Given the use of the mandatory term "shall," the structure of Section 1225(b) as a whole, and the defined exceptions to the initiation of removal proceedings located in Sections 1225(b)(2)(B) and (C), the Court finds that Section 1225(b)(2)(A) imposes a mandatory duty on immigration officers to initiate removal proceedings whenever they encounter an "applicant for admission" who "is not clearly and beyond a doubt entitled to be admitted.").

[143] Id. at 59.

[144] Crane v. Napolitano, 2013 U.S. Dist. LEXIS 187005 (N.D. TX, July 31, 2013).

[145] 5 U.S.C. §706(2)(A)("The reviewing court shall...hold unlawful and set aside agency action, findings, and conclusions found to be—arbitrary and capricious, an abuse of discretion, or otherwise not in accordance with law...").

[146] 421 U.S. 560, 571 (1975).

[147] Id. (citing DeVito v. Shultz, 300 F. Supp. 381, 383 (D.D.C. 1969)).

[148] Id. at 574.

[149] Id. at 573.

[150] Id. (citing DeVito v. Shultz, 72 L. R. R. M. 2682, 2683 (DC 1969)).

[151] Heckler, 470 U.S. at 833 n.4 (citing Adams v. Richardson, 480 F.2d 1159 (D.C. Cir. 1973)).

[152] Id.

[153] 480 F.2d 1159 (1973).

[154] Rather than invoking formal enforcement procedures, the agency had been pursuing voluntary compliance. The court held that the agency's reliance on voluntary compliance was inadequate:

The Act sets forth two alternative courses of action by which enforcement may be effected. In order to avoid unnecessary invocation of formal enforcement procedures, it includes the proviso that the institution must first be notified and given a chance to comply voluntarily. Although the Act does not provide a specific limit to the time period within which voluntary compliance may be sought, it is clear that a request for voluntary compliance, if not followed by responsive action on the part of the institution within a reasonable time, does not relieve the agency of the responsibility to enforce Title VI by one of the two alternative means contemplated by the statute. A consistent failure to do so is a dereliction of duty reviewable in the courts.

Id. at 1163.

[155] 42 U.S.C. §2000d-1.

[156] Adams v. Richardson, 351 F. Supp. 636, 641 (D.D.C. 1972).

[157] Id. at n.2 ("In the present case, the Court feels that ordering the Secretary of HEW to commence enforcement proceedings is not only appropriate but, indeed, required by the statute.").

[158] Adams v. Richardson, 480 F.2d 1159, 1162 (1973). Although affirming most of the lower court opinion, the appellate court modified the district court's order as applied to higher education facilities.

[159] Id.

[160] Id. The court also noted that HEW was playing an affirmative role in the violation of federal law by "actively supplying segregated institutions with federal funds." Id.

[161] Id. at 1163.

[162] Id. at 1162.

[163] Id.

[164] See, e.g., Dunlop, 421 U.S. at 574 (1975) ("The Secretary himself suggests that the rare case that might justify review beyond the confines of the reasons statement might arise, for example, 'if the Secretary were to declare that he no longer would enforce Title IV, or otherwise completely abrogate his enforcement responsibilities ... [or] if the Secretary prosecuted complaints in a constitutionally discriminatory manner ... .' Other cases might be imagined where the Secretary's decision would be 'plainly beyond the bounds of the Act [or] clearly defiant of the Act.' Since it inevitably would be a matter of grave public concern were a case to arise where the complaining member's proofs sufficed to require judicial inquiry into allegations of that kind, we may hope that such cases would be rare indeed.")(citations omitted); Northern Indiana Public Service Co. v. Federal Energy Regulatory Com., 782 F.2d 730, 745, 1986 (7th Cir. 1986) ("We do not think that the Commission can essentially abandon its regulatory function of ensuring just, reasonable, and preferential rates to Natural under the guise of unreviewable agency inaction.").

[165] In considering whether the abdication standard has been met, one legal commentator has suggested that a focus on the "sheer magnitude" of the agencies nonenforcement would be misplaced, noting that "to conclude that abdication has occurred, it may [] be necessary to find that the refusal to act applies in a large number of cases weighed against the total jurisdiction of the agency under the relevant statute." Cass Sunstein, Reviewing Agency Inaction After Heckler v. Chaney, 52 U. Chi. L. Rev. 653, 679 (1985).

[166] 106 F.3d 661 (5th Cir. 1997).

[167] Id. at 667.

[168] Id. See also, Myers v. U.S., 272 U.S. 52, 292 (1926)(Brandeis, J. dissenting) ("The President performs his full constitutional duty, if, with the means and instruments provided by Congress and within the limitations prescribed by it, he uses his best endeavors to secure the faithful execution of the laws enacted.").

[169] 779 F.2d 683, 685 (D.C. Cir. 1985).

[170] Id. at 685.

[171] Id. at 686-87 ("The FDA's action here was simply an exercise of its 'complete discretion . . . to decide how and when to enforce the Act.'").

[172] See, CRS Report R43013, Administrative Agencies and Claims of Unreasonable Delay: Analysis of Court Treatment, by Daniel T. Shedd.

[173] Med. Comm. for Human Rights v. SEC, 432 F.2d 659, 673 (D.C. Cir. 1970).

[174] Heckler, 470 U.S. at 839 (Brennan, J., concurring).

[175] 37 F.3d 671, 676 (D.C. Cir. 1994).

[176] Id. at 676-77.

[177] Id. at 677 (citations omitted).

[178] 497 F.2d 676, 679 n.19 (D.C. Cir. 1974) ("It would seem to follow that the exercise of prosecutorial discretion, like the exercise of Executive discretion generally, is subject to statutory and constitutional limits enforceable through judicial review.").

[179] Id. at 679.

[180] Id. (citations omitted).

[181] In re Aiken County, 645 F.3d 428, 436 (D.C. Cir. 2011).

[182] See, Powell v. Katzenbach, 359 F.2d 234, 234-35 (D.C. Cir. 1965) (citing Confiscation Cases, 74 U.S. (7 Wall.) 454, 19 L.Ed. 196 (1868); Moses v. Katzenbach, 119 U.S.App.D.C. 352, 342 F.2d 931 (1965), affirming sub nom. Moses v. Kennedy, 219 F.Supp. 762 (D.D.C. 1963); Goldberg v. Hoffman, 225 F.2d 463 (7th Cir. 1955); Pugach v. Klein, 193 F.Supp. 630 (S.D. N.Y.1961); United States v. Brokaw, 60 F.Supp. 100 (S.D. Ill. 1945).

[183] Powell, 359 F.2d at 234.

[184] 821 F.2d 1484 (11th Cir. 1987).

[185] Id. at 1489.

[186] Id. at 1490.

[187] Id. at n.3.

[188] 8 Op. O.L.C. 101, 126 (1984) ("In these cases the courts accepted jurisdiction to rule whether an entire enforcement program was being implemented based on an improper reading of the law.").

[189] Switchmen's Union of North America v. National Mediation Bd., 320 U.S. 297, 301 (1943).

[190] Heckler, 470 U.S. at 833.

[191] The DOJ has acknowledged that "prosecutorial discretion may be regulated to a certain extent by Congress..." 8 Op. Off. Legal Counsel 101, 126 (1984).

[192] See also, Nader v. Saxbe, 497 F. 2d 676, 679 n. 19 (D.C. Cir. 1974) ("It would seem to follow that the exercise of prosecutorial discretion, like the exercise of Executive discretion generally, is subject to statutory and constitutional limits enforceable through judicial review.").

[193] 222 U.S. 274 (1911).

[194] Pure Food and Drug Act §5 (1906).

[195] Morgan, 222 U.S. at 281.

[196] Id. Post Morgan, lower courts have hesitated to address whether Congress can simply remove enforcement discretion from executive branch officers by federal law, instead interpreting statutory provisions so as not to remove enforcement discretion. In Inmates of Attica, 477 F. 2d 375 (2nd Cir. 1973), the Second Circuit found the language of 42 U.S.C. §1987 insufficient to establish "an intent by congress to depart so significantly from the normal assumption of executive discretion." As a result, the court determined that it "therefore becomes unnecessary to decide whether, if Congress were by explicit direction and guidelines to remove all prosecutorial discretion with respect to certain crimes or in certain circumstances we would properly direct that a prosecution be undertaken." The Fifth Circuit noted similar concerns in U.S. v. Cox, 342 F.2d 167, 172 (5th Cir. 1965), warning that "[i]f it were not for the discretionary power given to the United States Attorney to prevent an indictment by withholding his signature, there might be doubt as to the constitutionality of the requirement of Rule 48 for leave of court for a dismissal of a pending prosecution." In a concurring opinion in Nathan v. Smith, 737 F.2d 1069, 1077 (D.C. Cir. 1984), Judge Bork similarly identified the "severity of the constitutional problem that would arise" were Congress to authorize the courts to direct the Attorney General in his law enforcement function.

[197] 74 U.S. 454 (1869).

[198] Price, supra note 1 at 715 ("Thus, in one of the canonical statements of executive authority over prosecution, the Court acknowledged congressional authority to override the executive branch's presumptive discretion to dismiss particular charges.").

[199] Confiscation Cases, 74 U.S. at 457.

[200] Heckler, 470 U.S. at 832 (1985); Community for Creative Non-Violence v. Pierce, 786 F.2d 1199, 1201 (D.C. Cir. 1986).

[201] Lincoln v. Vigil, 508 U.S. 182, 193 (1993) ("Congress may always circumscribe agency discretion to allocate resources by putting restrictions in the operative statutes..."). Congress enjoys near plenary authority over the administrative state. Indeed, a federal agency "literally has no power to act...unless and until Congress confers power upon it." La. Public Serv. Com v. FCC, 476 U.S. 355, 374 (1986); Friends of the Crystal River v. EPA, 35 F.3d

1073, 1080 (6th Cir. 1994) (noting that "agencies are creatures of statutory authority. Thus, they have no power to act ... unless and until Congress confers power upon them.").

[202] Heckler, 470 U.S.at 847 (Marshall, J. concurring).

[203] Riley v. St. Luke's Episcopal Hosp., 252 F.3d 749 (5th Cir. 2001).

[204] The qui tam provision of the False Claims Act, which allows a private individual to institute a civil suit on behalf of the government, is discussed in greater detail infra.

[205] Riley, 252 F.3d at 755.

[206] Id. at 756.

[207] Id. at 755.

[208] 8 Op. Off. Legal Counsel 101, 115 (1984) ("neither the Judicial nor Legislative Branches may directly interfere with the prosecutorial discretion of the Executive by directing the Executive Branch to prosecute particular individuals.").

[209] This general principle has limited exceptions. Congress, may for example, unilaterally enforce contempts against its own proceedings under the inherent contempt power. See, McGrain v. Daugherty, 273 U.S. 135 (1927).

[210] Springer v. Philippine Islands, 277 U.S. 189, 202 (1927).

[211] The Federalist Papers, No. 47, at 301 (J. Madison)(C. Rossiter ed. 1961). Madison adopted Montesquieu's admonition that "[t]here can be no liberty where the legislative and executive powers are united in the same person, or body of magistrates." See, CRS Legal Sidebar, Separating Power: Ancient Roots and Philosophical Origins, by Todd Garvey.

[212] See, e.g., Buckley v. Valeo, 424 U.S. 1 (1976); Bowsher v. Synar, 478 U.S. 714 (1986).

[213] Myers v. U.S., 272 U.S. 52 (1926). An exception to this principle was established in Young v. United States ex rel. Vuitton, 481 U.S.787 (1987). In that case, a district court appointed private attorneys as special counsel to prosecute a criminal contempt of court citation against a party that had violated a court injunction. For a discussion of the case and its application to the President's enforcement power see, Todd D. Peterson, Prosecuting Executive Branch Officials for Contempt of Congress, 66 N.Y.U. L. Rev. 563 (1991).

[214] Morrison v. Olson, 487 U.S. 654 (1988).

[215] 418 U.S. 683, 693 (1974); Heckler, 470 U.S. at 832.

[216] See, e.g., 8 Op. Off. Legal Counsel 101, (1984).

[217] U.S. Const, Art I §9 cl.3 ("No Bill of Attainder or ex post facto Law shall be passed."). See also, CRS Report R40826, Bills of Attainder: The Constitutional Implications of Congress Legislating Narrowly, by Kenneth R. Thomas. A bill of attainder generally has been described as a law "that legislatively determines guilt and inflicts punishment upon an identifiable individual without provision of the protections of a judicial trial." Nixon v. Administrator of General Services, 433 U.S. 425, 468 (1977) (emphasis added). Under a compelled prosecution statute, an individual would arguably only be punished after being found guilty in a judicial trial.

[218] Inmates of Attica, 477 F. 2d at 375 ("[F]ederal courts have traditionally and, to our knowledge, uniformly refrained from overturning...discretionary decisions of federal prosecuting authorities not to prosecute..."); Powell v. Katzenbach, 359 F.2d 234 (D.C. Cir. 1965) ("[I]t is well settled that the question of whether and when prosecution is to be instituted is within the discretion of the Attorney General. Mandamus will not lie to control the exercise of this discretion."); Pugach v. Klein, 193 F. Supp. 630, 634 (S.D. N.Y. 1961)("All of these considerations point up the wisdom of vesting broad discretion in the United States Attorney. The federal courts are powerless to interfere with his discretionary power. The Court cannot compel him to prosecute a complaint, or even an indictment, whatever his

reasons for not acting. The remedy for any dereliction of his duty lies, not with the courts, but, with the executive branch of our government and ultimately with the people.").

[219] 487 U.S. 654 (1988).

[220] 28 U.S.C. §§591 et seq.

[221] 28 U.S.C. §591.

[222] 28 U.S.C. §592.

[223] 28 U.S.C. §594; 28 U.S.C. §596. The role of Congress under the independent counsel law was very limited. Under the law, Congress could not order the appointment of a prosecutor or independent counsel, but majorities of either party within the House or Senate Judiciary Committees could have requested action by the Attorney General. 28 U.S.C. §592(g)(1). The Attorney General was not required to apply for the appointment of an independent counsel in response to such congressional request; and if the Attorney General did not make such application, he or she was directed merely to respond to Congress with the reasons an independent counsel was not appointed. 28 U.S.C. §592(g)(2), (3).

[224] Morrison, 487 U.S. at 668-89.

[225] In discussing the removal question, the Court acknowledged that "[t]here is no real dispute that the functions performed by the independent counsel are 'executive' in the sense that they are law enforcement functions that typically have been undertaken by officials within the Executive Branch." Id. at 691. But the court could not "see how the President's need to control the exercise of that discretion is so central to the functioning of the Executive Branch as to require as a matter of constitutional law that the counsel be terminable at will by the President." Id. at 691-92. The Court concluded that the "for cause" removal restrictions, did not "sufficiently deprive[] the President of control over the independent counsel" such that it would "interfere impermissibly with his constitutional obligation to ensure the faithful execution of the laws." Id. at 693.

[226] Id. at 695 (citing CFTC v. Schor, 478 U.S. 833, 856 (1986)); Nixon v. Administrator of General Services, 433 U.S. 425, 443 (1977).

[227] Id. at 694.

[228] Id. at 695.

[229] Id. at 696.

[230] Id.

[231] Id. at 706 (Scalia, J. dissenting). An equally robust approach to prosecutorial discretion and the President's enforcement power was taken by Judge Kavanaugh in his concurring opinion in In re Aiken County, 725 F. 3d 255 (D.C. Cir. 2013) (connecting the President's exercise of prosecutorial discretion to the pardon power).

[232] Id. at 711.

[233] Id. at 710.

[234] Id. at 695 (emphasis added).

[235] Id. at 695-96.

[236] For a general discussion of qui tam actions see CRS Report R40785, Qui Tam: The False Claims Act and Related Federal Statutes, by Charles Doyle.

[237] 31 U.S.C. §3730.

[238] 31 U.S.C. §3730(b).

[239] 31 U.S.C. §3730(c).

[240] Id.

[241] United States ex rel. Stone v. Rockwell International Corp., 282 F.3d 787, 805-807 (10th Cir. 2002); Riley v. St. Luke's Episcopal Hospital, 252 F.3d 749, 757 (5th Cir. 2001)(en banc) ("Any intrusion by the qui tam relator in the Executive's Article II power is comparatively

modest, especially given the control mechanisms inherent in the FCA to mitigate such an intrusion and the civil context in which qui tam suits are pursued. Hence, the qui tam portions of the FCA do not violate the constitutional doctrine of separation of powers by impinging upon the Executive's constitutional duty to take care that the laws are faithfully executed under Article II of the Constitution"); United States ex rel. Taxpayers Against Fraud v. General Electric Co., 41 F.3d 1032, 1041 (6th Cir. 1995); United States ex rel. Kelly v. Boeing Co., 9 F.3d 743, 757 (9th Cir. 1993) ("Taken as a whole, and considering the removal issue in particular, the FCA affords the Executive Branch a degree of control over qui tam relators that is not distinguishable from the degree of control the Morrison Court found the Executive Branch exercises over independent counsels").

[242] United States ex rel. Kelly v. Boeing Co., 9 F.3d 743, 754-55 (9th Cir. 1993)(emphasis added); United States ex rel. Taxpayers Against Fraud v. General Electric Co., 41 F.3d 1032, 1041 (6th Cir. 1994).

[243] Congress arguably has a variety of options available to it in attempting to counter executive nonenforcement. In addition to enacting legislation that confines the discretion to determine whether to initiate an enforcement action in response to a violation of federal law, it could be argued that Congress may also utilize its power of the purse to encourage enforcement by the executive; directly reject, through the Congressional Review Act or otherwise, agency nonenforcement guidance documents; assign enforcement powers to independent agencies that are not subject to Presidential control; amend the APA to clarify that certain administrative nonenforcement decisions are not "committed to agency discretion" and subject to judicial review; encourage the assistance of states in the enforcement of federal law; or authorize private citizens to initiate enforcement actions on behalf of the United States. The constitutionality of these proposed alternatives will not be addressed in this report. See also, U.S. v. Windsor, 133 S. Ct. 2675, 2704-05 (2013) (Scalia, J., dissenting) ("if majorities in both Houses of Congress care enough about the matter...[Congress has] available inumerable ways to compel executive action without a lawsuit...").

[244] Motor Vehicle Mfrs. Ass'n v. State Farm Mut. Auto. Ins. Co., 463 U.S. 29, 43 (1983).

[245] Heckler, 470 U.S. at 833.

[246] 437 U.S. 153, 174 (1978)(holding that Congress intended endangered species "to be afforded the highest of priorities.").

[247] Id. at 194. The language from TVA pertained to situations when enforcement was "sought" as opposed to nonenforcement.

[248] If a court were to compel a prosecution any number of practical questions would need to be considered:

Nor is it clear what the judiciary's role of supervision should be were it to undertake such a review. At what point would the prosecutor be entitled to call a halt to further investigation as unlikely to be productive? What evidentiary standard would be used to decide whether prosecution should be compelled? How much judgment would the United States Attorney be allowed? Would he be permitted to limit himself to a strong 'test' case rather than pursue weaker cases? What collateral factors would be permissible bases for a decision not to prosecute, e. g., the pendency of another criminal proceeding elsewhere against the same parties? What sort of review should be available in cases like the present one where the conduct complained of allegedly violates state as well as federal laws? With limited personnel and facilities at his disposal, what priority would the prosecutor be required to give to cases in which investigation or prosecution was directed by the court?

See, Inmates of Attica Correctional Facility v. Rockefeller, 477 F. 2d 375, 380 (2nd Cir. 1973) (citations omitted).

[249] See supra note 196.

[250] 418 U.S. 683, 693 (1974).

[251] See, e.g., Heckler, 470 U.S. at 733 (Marshall J. concurring):

> The half-sentence cited from Nixon, which states that the Executive has "absolute discretion to decide whether to prosecute a case," 418 U. S., at 693, is the only apparent support the Court actually offers for even the limited notion that prosecutorial discretion in the criminal area is unreviewable. But that half-sentence is of course misleading, for Nixon held it an abuse of that discretion to attempt to exercise it contrary to validly promulgated regulations. Thus, Nixon actually stands for a very different proposition than the one for which the Court cites it: faced with a specific claim of abuse of prosecutorial discretion, Nixon makes clear that courts are not powerless to intervene.

[252] See, Peterson, supra note 213 at 612 (arguing that the Constitution does not permit Congress to compel a criminal prosecution)("Congress cannot both pass the laws and decide who shall be prosecuted for their violation.").

[253] 2 U.S.C. §194 (providing that the President of the Senate or the Speaker of the House shall certify the contempt "to the appropriate United States attorney, whose duty it shall be to bring the matter before the grand jury for its action.")

[254] 8 Op. Off. Legal Counsel 101, 126 (1984).

[255] Id. at 127. For a discussion of the myriad issues associated with the criminal contempt provision, including judicial treatment of the U.S. Attorneys obligations under 2 U.S.C. §194 see CRS Report RL34097, Congress's Contempt Power and the Enforcement of Congressional Subpoenas: Law, History, Practice, and Procedure, by Todd Garvey and Alissa M. Dolan. See, Ex parte Frankfeld, 32 F. Supp 915, 916 (D.D.C. 1940) ("It seems quite apparent that Congress intended to leave no measure of discretion to either the Speaker of the House or the President of the Senate, under such circumstances, but made the certification of facts to the district attorney a mandatory proceeding, and it left no discretion with the district attorney as to what he should do about it. He is required, under the language of the statute, to submit the facts to the grand jury.) (emphasis added); But see, Wilson v. U.S., 369 F.2d 198 (D.C. Cir. 1966) (determining the Speakers duty under the statute to be discretionary).

[256] But see, Riley v. St. Luke's Episcopal Hosp., 252 F.2d 749, 755-56 (holding Morrison inapplicable in the civil context).

[257] Morrison v. Olson 487 U.S. 654, 685-97 (1988).

[258] "It is this concern of encroachment and aggrandizement that has animated our separation-of-powers jurisprudence and aroused our vigilance against the 'hydraulic pressure inherent within each of the separate Branches to exceed the outer limits of its power.'" Mistretta v. U.S., 488 U.S. 361, 382 (1989). In Free Enterprise Fund v. PCAOB, the Court determined that Congress had "deprive[d] the President of adequate control over" the Public Company Accounting Oversight Board (Board) by insulating Board members from Presidential control with dual layers of "for cause" removal protections. The added layer of tenure protection "impaired" the President from "holding his subordinates accountable for their conduct." 561 U.S. 477, 130 S. Ct. 3138, 3154, 3160 (2010).

[259] Morrison, at 695 ("It is undeniable that the Act reduces the amount of control or supervision that the Attorney General and, through him, the President exercises over the investigation and prosecution of a certain class of alleged criminal activity."); United States ex rel. Kelly v. Boeing Co., 9 F.3d 743, 754-55 (9th Cir. 1993)("Likewise, we do not deny that the qui tam provisions of the FCA to some degree diminish Executive Branch control over the initiation and prosecution of a defined class of civil litigation.").

[260] It is important to reiterate that if the executive branch failed to comply with such a law, it is unlikely that a court would directly order a federal prosecutor to commence a specific prosecution. Thus, while such a law may be within Congress's authority to enact, it may not be within the courts authority to enforce.

[261] The Secretary retained significant discretion to determine whether the precondition to the required enforcement action was met. The Secretary's obligation was only triggered where he determined that there was "probable cause" to believe that a violation occurred. Dunlop v. Bachowski, 421 US. 560, 563 n.2 (1975).

[262] Heckler, 470 U.S. at 834.

[263] Id.

[264] Id. at 834-35.

[265] Dunlop, 421 U.S. U.S. at 572-73.

[266] Id. at 574.

[267] Id. at 575-76.

[268] Id. at 576 n.12.

[269] Id.

[270] Bachowski v. Brennan, 405 F. Supp. 1227 (W.D. PA 1975).

In: Delay and Discretion …
Editor: Cory Derricks

ISBN: 978-1-63463-482-3

Chapter 4

IMPLEMENTING THE AFFORDABLE CARE ACT: DELAYS, EXTENSIONS, AND OTHER ACTIONS TAKEN BY THE ADMINISTRATION*

C. Stephen Redhead and Janet Kinzer

INTRODUCTION

The two federal agencies primarily responsible for administering the private health insurance provisions in the Patient Protection and Affordable Care Act (ACA)—the Centers for Medicare & Medicaid Services (CMS) within the Department of Health and Human Services (HHS), and the Internal Revenue Service (IRS) within the Treasury Department—have taken certain actions to delay, extend, or otherwise modify the law's implementation.[1]

Table 1 summarizes selected administrative actions taken by CMS and the IRS to address ACA implementation. The table entries, which are grouped under general topic headings, are not organized in any particular priority order. Each entry includes a brief summary of the action and some accompanying explanatory material and comments to help provide additional context. Where available, links are provided to relevant regulatory and guidance documents

---

* This is an edited, reformatted and augmented version of a Congressional Research Service publication R43474, prepared for Members and Committees of Congress dated August 1, 2014.

online. Readers are encouraged to review these documents for more details about each action taken.

A companion CRS report summarizes all the *legislative* actions taken by Congress since the ACA's enactment to repeal, defund, delay, or otherwise amend the law.[2]

ACTIONS ADDRESS KEY ELEMENTS OF THE ACA

The actions summarized in *Table 1*, which address some of the ACA's core insurance expansion provisions,[3] are not the result of a single policy decision. They represent multiple separate decisions taken by the Administration to address a variety of factors affecting the implementation of specific provisions of the law. In compiling the table, CRS made decisions about which administrative actions to include, and which ones to leave out. Generally, CRS included the more significant actions that have been the subject of debate among health policy analysts and, in some instances, the target of criticism by opponents of the ACA. The table is not intended to be a comprehensive list of ACA-related administrative actions.

Employer Mandate Delays

Perhaps the most controversial action is the Administration's decision to delay enforcement of the ACA's "employer mandate." On July 9, 2013, the IRS announced that it would not take enforcement action against employers who fail to comply with the law's employer mandate until the beginning of 2015. This ACA provision, which took effect on January 1, 2014, requires employers with 50 or more full-time equivalent employees to offer their full-time workers affordable health coverage or pay a penalty if one or more employees purchase coverage through an exchange and receive a premium tax credit. The IRS subsequently announced that employers with at least 50 but fewer than 100 full-time equivalent employees will have an additional year to comply with the employer mandate. According to the Administration, these actions were taken after it concluded that the ACA's employer mandate could not be enforced until the related requirement that employers report the coverage they offer to their employees had been fully implemented. The IRS says that it is working with stakeholders to simplify the reporting process consistent with effective implementation of the law.[4]

Renewal of Noncompliant Plans

Other controversial administrative actions include those taken in response to the decision by insurers to cancel individual and small-group health plans that do not meet the ACA's new standards for health insurance coverage, which also took effect on January 1, 2014. On November 14, 2013, the Administration notified state insurance commissioners of the option to delay enforcement of certain health insurance reforms under the ACA. It encouraged state officials to permit insurers to renew noncompliant policies in the individual and small-group market for policy years starting between January 1, 2104, and October 1, 2014.[5] The Administration has since extended this policy for two years. Thus, at the option of state regulators, insurers may continue to renew noncompliant policies at any time through October 1, 2016.[6]

Special Enrollment Periods and Hardship Exemptions

Finally, HHS has been criticized for providing a special enrollment period for individuals who were unable to enroll in a qualified health plan (QHP) offered through a federally facilitated exchange prior to the March 31, 2014, deadline due to technical problems or other exceptional circumstances.[7] The special enrollment period allows the individuals to enroll in a QHP after the 2014 open enrollment period closes. These individuals were also granted a hardship exemption from the ACA's "individual mandate" penalty. Under the law, most U.S. citizens and legal residents are required to maintain ACA-compliant health coverage beginning in 2014. Those without coverage for three consecutive months are subject to a penalty unless they qualify for one of the statutory exemptions or are covered under a hardship exemption established by CMS.

Arguments for and Against the Administrative Actions

Opponents of the ACA, who believe that the law is fundamentally flawed, argue that some of the Administration's actions effectively rewrite the law in an effort to make it work and confuse the public. The ACA's critics also assert that the actions taken by the Administration to delay enforcement of the employer mandate are illegal and raise concerns that the President is not upholding his constitutional duty to faithfully execute federal law.[8]

The Administration counters that its actions are not a refusal to implement and enforce the ACA as written. Instead, they represent temporary corrections necessary to ensure the effective implementation of a very large and complex law. Agency officials point to a number of factors that have made it difficult to meet various ACA deadlines. Those factors include a lack of appropriations to help fund implementation activities, technological problems including the poorly managed launch of the websites for the federally facilitated exchange and the state-based exchanges, and the need to phase in the various interconnected parts of the law so as to avoid unnecessary disruption of employment and insurance markets.[9]

Regarding the employer mandate delay, the Administration says that its actions are no different from those taken by previous administrations faced with the challenges of implementing a complicated law. The Administration notes that its decision to grant employers "transition relief," taken pursuant to administrative authority under the Internal Revenue Code to "prescribe all needful rules and regulations" to administer tax laws,[10] is part of an established practice to provide relief to taxpayers who might otherwise struggle to comply with new tax law.[11]

Notwithstanding the Administration's arguments, critics question whether some of the recent delays of ACA provisions exceed the executive's traditional discretion in enforcing law to the point that they represent a blatant disregard of the law. For example, they argue that the decision to encourage states to allow insurers to renew noncompliant policies for people who want to keep their current plans directly contravenes provisions of the ACA that had become politically inconvenient.[12]

CONGRESSIONAL LAWSUIT

On July 30, 2014, the House voted 225-201 to approve a resolution (H.Res. 676) authorizing litigation "for actions by the President or other executive branch officials inconsistent with their duties under the Constitution of the United States."[13] The resolution authorizes Speaker John Boehner to sue the Obama Administration on behalf of the House of Representatives over implementation of the private health insurance provisions (i.e., Title I) of the ACA. The Speaker has indicated that any such lawsuit would specifically challenge the Administration's delay of the ACA employer mandate. "In 2013, the President changed the health care law without a vote of Congress, effectively creating his own law by literally waiving the employer mandate and the penalties for failing to comply with it," said Mr. Boehner.[14]

Table 1. Selected Administrative Delays and Other Changes to ACA Implementation

Summary of Administrative Action	Explanatory Notes and Comments
Hardship Exemptions and Special Enrollment Periods	
On October 28, 2013, CMS announced a hardship exemption from the individual mandate penalty for individuals who waited until after February 15, 2014, to enroll in a qualified health plan (QHP) offered through an exchange during the 2014 open enrollment period. See http://www.cms.gov/CCIIO/Resources/Fact-Sheets-and-FAQs/Downloads/enrollment-period-faq-10-28-2013.pdf. [Note: HHS followed that action with additional announcements aimed at individuals seeking to enroll for coverage beginning January 1, 2014. For example, on November 22, 2013, HHS extended the December 15 deadline to sign up for health coverage beginning January 1 by eight days, to December 23. Citing delays due to heavy use of Healthcare.gov, HHS on December 23 announced a 24-hour grace period for individuals trying to sign up for coverage beginning January 1, effectively extending the deadline to December 24. For more information, see http://www.nytimes.com/interactive/2013/12/20/us/politics/changes-and-delays-to-health-law.html?_r=1&.]	ACA Section 1501(b) requires most U.S. citizens and legal residents to maintain minimum essential coverage (MEC) beginning in 2014. Individuals without coverage for three consecutive months will have to pay a penalty unless they qualify for one of the statutory exemptions or are covered under a hardship exemption established by CMS. CMS specified in regulation (45 C.F.R. 155.410) that the initial open enrollment period for individuals to enroll in coverage through an exchange would extend from October 1, 2013, through March 31, 2014. For individuals who sign up for coverage between the 1st and 15th of a given month, the coverage effective date is the first day of the immediately following month. However, for those who sign up between the 16th and end of a given month, the coverage effective date is the first day of the second following month. Thus, an individual who signed up on February 16, 2014, would not be insured until April 1, 2014. That individual would be uninsured for the first three months of 2014 and would have to pay a fine, unless otherwise exempt. CMS exercised its authority under IRC Section 5000A(e)(5), as added by ACA Section 1501(b), to establish a hardship exemption in order to provide relief for such individuals who waited until after February 15, 2014, to enroll.

Table 1. (Continued)

Summary of Administrative Action	Explanatory Notes and Comments
On March 26, 2014, five days prior to the close of the 2014 open enrollment period, CMS announced that people who attested that they were unable to enroll in a QHP through the federally facilitated exchange for various specified circumstances would be eligible for a special enrollment period (pursuant to ACA Section 1311(c)(6)(C), as implemented by 45 C.F.R. 155.420) enabling them to enroll after open enrollment closed on March 31. These individuals also were eligible for a hardship exemption for the months prior to the effective date of their coverage, because they were treated as if they had enrolled in coverage by March 31. On May 2, 2014, CMS announced a comparable hardship exemption for all the months prior to the effective date of coverage for those individuals who obtained MEC effective on or before May 1, 2014, outside of an exchange. On May 2, 2014, CMS also announced (1) a special enrollment period through July 1, 2014, for individuals eligible for or enrolled in COBRA continuation coverage, giving them the option of enrolling in a qualified health plan through a federally facilitated exchange; (2) a special enrollment period for individuals whose individual health plans are up for renewal, giving them the option of enrolling in a qualified health plan through a federally facilitated exchange; and (3) special enrollment periods and hardship exemptions for individuals beginning or ending their service in AmeriCorps, VISTA, or the National Civilian Community Corps (NCCC). For more information, see http://www.cms.gov/CCIIO/Resources/Regulations-and-Guidance/Downloads/SEPand-hardship-FAQ-5-1-2014.pdf.	The circumstances that warrant a special enrollment period include a natural disaster, a serious medical condition, unresolved casework, errors related to immigration status, and technical problems with Healthcare.gov. For a complete list, see http://www.cms.gov/CCIIO/Resources/Regulations-and-Guidance/Downloads/complex-cases-SEP-3-26-2014.pdf. State-based exchanges are encouraged to adopt similar special enrollment periods to the ones established for federally facilitated exchanges.
State-Based Exchanges and Retroactive Payment of Subsidies	

Summary of Administrative Action	Explanatory Notes and Comments
On February 27, 2014, CMS issued guidance allowing state-based exchanges to provide advance payments of the premium tax credit and cost-sharing reductions on a retroactive basis for eligible individuals who were unable to enroll in a QHP through the exchange because IT problems prevented timely eligibility determinations. CMS considers this situation an exceptional circumstance under 45 C.F.R. 155.420. Once a successful eligibility determination is obtained and the individual enrolls in the QHP through the exchange, the exchange may deem the coverage to have started on the date the individual originally submitted an application and encountered the IT problems. This would allow the individual to get the premium tax credit and cost-sharing reductions retroactively if they qualify based on income.	Individuals must receive an eligibility determination in order to enroll in a QHP offered through an exchange and receive the premium tax credit and cost-sharing reductions authorized by the ACA.
Additionally, if an individual covered under this exceptional circumstance has enrolled in the QHP outside of the exchange, then once that individual receives an eligibility determination for exchange coverage, the exchange may deem the individual to have been enrolled in the QHP through the exchange retroactive to the date the individual enrolled outside of the exchange. Again, this would allow the individual to get the premium tax credit and cost-sharing reductions retroactively if he or she qualifies based on income. Upon making an eligibility determination, the exchange also must provide a special enrollment period under 45 C.F.R. 155.420 to allow these individuals the opportunity to change QHPs prospectively.	The February 27, 2014, guidance is at http://www.cms.gov/CCIIO/Resources/Regulations-and-Guidance/Downloads/retroactive-advance-payments-ptc-csrs-02-27- 14.pdf. CMS issued clarifications to the February 27 guidance on March 14; see http://www.cms.gov/CCIIO/Resources/Fact-Sheets-and-FAQs/Downloads/retroactive-advance-payments-ptc-csrs-03-14-14.pdf.
Renewal of Noncompliant Health Plans	
On November 14, 2013, the Administration established a transition policy—which it encouraged state insurance commissioners to adopt—in response to the decision of insurers to send cancellation notices to individuals and small businesses with health plans in the	Under the ACA, health plans that consumers had at the time the law was enacted in 2010 were "grandfathered" in and have existed largely unchanged since the law's enactment. Grandfathered plans do not have to adopt many of the ACA's new

Table 1. (Continued)

Summary of Administrative Action	Explanatory Notes and Comments
individual and small group markets that did not meet the ACA's new standards for health insurance coverage. Under the policy, insurers could choose to renew such noncompliant health plans for a policy year starting between January 1, 2014, and October 1, 2014, if permitted by state regulators. CMS also indicated that it would consider the impact of this transition policy in assessing whether to extend it. The intent of the policy was to allow Americans whose insurance companies cancelled their insurance coverage for 2014 to remain in their plans. See http://www.whitehouse. gov/the-press-office/2013/11/14/fact-sheet-new-administrationproposal-help-consumers-facing-cancellatio. On December 19, 2013, CMS issued further clarification of the options available to consumers with cancelled policies. These consumers are eligible for a hardship exemption from the individual mandate pcnalty if othcr availablc options arc unaffordable, or they can purchase a catastrophic plan if one is offered in their area. See http://www.cms.gov/CCIIO/ Resources/Regulations-and-Guidance/Downloads/ cancellation-consumer-options-12-19-2013.pdf.	requirements for health insurance, including coverage of essential health benefits and other consumer protections that took effect at the beginning of 2014. However, new (i.e., non-grandfathered) plans purchased since the law's enactment have to meet all the ACA requirements. For a January 8, 2014, update on state decisions regarding the transition policy on health plan cancellations, see http://www.commonwealthfund.org/ Blog/2013/Nov/State-Decisions-on-Policy-Cancellations-Fix.aspx.
On March 5, 2014, CMS extended the transition policy for two years, to policy years beginning on or before October 1, 2016. Thus, at the option of state regulators, insurers who issued (or plan to issue) a policy in the individual or small group market under the November 14, 2013, transition policy may renew such policies at any time through October 1, 2016. CMS also indicated that it would consider the impact of the two-year extension in assessing whether an additional one-year extension is appropriate. CMS also extended the hardship	

Summary of Administrative Action	Explanatory Notes and Comments
exemption established for consumers with cancelled policies until October 1, 2016. See http://www.cms.gov/CCIIO/Resources/Regulations-and-Guidance/Downloads/transition-to-compliant-policies-03- 06-2015.pdf.	
Exchange Applicant Eligibility and Verification	
HHS's July 15, 2013, final rule on health insurance exchange eligibility and enrollment included two, one-year delays regarding verification of applicant information. First, the rule permits state-based exchanges during 2014 to audit fewer than 100% of exchange applicants who report income at least 10% below the amount indicated by IRS and SSA records, provided the sample size used is statistically significant. The government initially had proposed an audit of all such individuals.	Under IRC Section 36B(b), as added by ACA Section 1401(a), individuals and families who enroll in qualified health plans (QHPs) offered through an exchange are eligible for refundable premium tax credits if their income is between 100% and 400% of the federal poverty level.
Second, state-based exchanges will not be required until 2015 to verify applicants' information about employer coverage in order to determine eligibility for premium tax credits. During 2014 the exchanges may accept an applicant's attestation regarding employer coverage without further verification. See 78 *Federal Register* 42159, http://www.gpo.gov/fdsys/pkg/FR-2013-07-15/pdf/2013-16271.pdf.	Under IRC Section 36B(c)(2)(C), as added by ACA Section 1401(a), individuals whose employer offers a health plan that is affordable (i.e., the employee's share of the premium does not exceed 9.5% of the employee's household income) and provides minimum value (i.e., the plan's share of the total allowed costs of benefits provided under the plan is at least 60%) are not eligible for a premium tax credit through the exchange.
2015 Open Enrollment	
On November 22, 2013, HHS announced that it was planning to delay by one month the open enrollment period for plan years that begin in 2015. The dates for the 2015 open enrollment period were included in the final rule for benefit and payment parameters for 2015, which was published on March 11, 2014. See 79 *Federal Register* 13743, http://www.gpo.gov/fdsys/pkg/FR-2014-03-11/pdf/2014-05052.pdf.	The open enrollment period for 2015 will begin November 15, 2014—instead of October 15, 2014—and extend through February 15, 2015.
Employer Mandate and Insurer Reporting	

Table 1. (Continued)

Summary of Administrative Action	Explanatory Notes and Comments
On July 9, 2013, the IRS provided transition relief to employers by delaying until 2015 the ACA requirement that employers with at least 50 full-time equivalent employees provide health coverage for their full-time workers or risk paying a penalty. The IRS also delayed until 2015 the requirement for employers and insurers to report certain information to the IRS. The agency indicated that these actions were taken pursuant to its administrative authority under IRC Section 7805(a) to grant transition relief when implementing new legislation. See http://www.irs.gov/pub/irs-drop/n-13-45.PDF. The IRS's February 12, 2014, final rule on the ACA's employer mandate included an additional year of transition relief for employers with at least 50 but fewer than 100 full-time equivalent employees, provided the employers meet certain other requirements such as not reducing their workforce to qualify for the additional relief and maintaining previously offered coverage. These employers would not be subject to the ACA's employer mandate until 2016. In addition, employers subject to the mandate in 2015 (i.e., those with 100 or more full-time equivalent employees) can avoid a penalty by offering coverage to at least 70% of their full-time employees, as opposed to 95% of such employees (as described in the explanatory notes). See 79 *Federal Register* 8543, http://www.gpo.gov/fdsys/pkg/FR-2014-02-12/pdf/2014-03082.pdf.	Generally, under IRC Section 4980H ("Shared Responsibility for Employers Regarding Health Coverage"), as added by ACA Section 1513, employers with at least 50 full-time equivalent employees are liable for a penalty if (1) they do not offer health coverage or they offer coverage to fewer than 95% of their full-time employees (and their dependents) and at least one full-time employee receives a premium tax credit for coverage purchased through an exchange; or (2) they offer health coverage to all or at least 95% of full-time employees, but at least one full-time employee receives a premium tax credit for coverage purchased through an exchange because the employer didn't offer coverage to that employee or because the coverage offered was either unaffordable or did not provide minimum value (see explanatory note for "Exchange Applicant Eligibility and Verification"). IRC Section 6055, as added by ACA Section 1502(a), requires reporting by insurers, self-insuring employers, and other parties that provide health coverage. IRC Section 6056, as added by ACA Section 1514(a), requires certain employers to report on the health coverage they offer to their full-time employees. For more information on the ACA employer mandate, including transition relief, see http://www.irs.gov/uac/Newsroom/Questions-and-Answers-on-Employer-Shared-Responsibility-Provisions-Under-the-Affordable-Care-Act.
W-2 Reporting of Employer-Sponsored Health Coverage	
In a series of notices, the IRS has provided transition relief to employers by giving them additional time to make any necessary changes to payroll systems and procedures	IRC Section 6051(a), as amended by ACA Section 9002, generally requires the cost of employer-sponsored health coverage to be reported on Form W-2 (Wage and Tax

Summary of Administrative Action	Explanatory Notes and Comments
in order to comply with the ACA's W-2 reporting requirement. First, it made reporting on the 2011 W-2—typically provided to employees in January 2012—optional. Second, while employers are generally required to report the cost of health benefits on the W-2 for 2012 and subsequent years, the IRS has provided transition relief for certain employers and with respect to certain types of coverage. Employers covered by the transition relief are not required to report until future guidance is issued.	Statement). This reporting requirement applies to taxable years beginning after December 31, 2010. For more information on the W-2 reporting requirement and associated transition relief, see http://www.irs.gov/uac/Employer-Provided-HealthCoverage-Informational-Reporting-Requirements:-Questions-and-Answers.
Annual Limits on Cost-Sharing and Deductibles	
Plans may use more than one service provider to help administer benefits (e.g., a separate pharmacy benefits manager for coverage of pharmaceuticals), each of which may impose different cost-sharing. To allow service providers more time to coordinate their cost-sharing requirements so that the plan meets the ACA's annual cost-sharing limits, the Administration on February 20, 2013, announced a one-year grace period to allow each service provider to apply the cost-sharing limits to the benefits they administer. Under this policy, for example, many group health plans will be able to maintain separate cost-sharing limits for medical coverage (e.g., hospital and doctors' services) and for prescription drug coverage. However, this policy applies only to the first plan year beginning in 2014. See http://www.dol.gov/ebsa/ faqs/faqaca12.html.	PHSA Section 2707(b), as added by ACA Section 1201, requires group health plans to ensure that any annual cost-sharing (e.g., deductibles, coinsurance, copayments) imposed under the plan for a plan year beginning on or after January 1, 2014, does not exceed the limitations established under ACA Section 1302(c)(1) and (c)(2). Under ACA Section 1302(c)(1), annual cost-sharing for a plan year beginning in 2014 may not exceed the current-law Health Savings Accounts limits; for each plan year thereafter these limits are indexed to the percentage increase in average per-capita premiums. Under ACA Section 1302(c)(2), which applies only to the small group market, the deductible for a plan year beginning in 2014 may not exceed $2,000 for individuals and $4,000 for families; again, for each plan year thereafter these limits are indexed to the percentage increase in average per-capita premiums.
Pre-Existing Condition Insurance Plan (PCIP)	
On March 14, 2014, HHS announced that individuals enrolled in a PCIP who had not yet found new health insurance coverage through an exchange could purchase an additional month of PCIP coverage through	ACA Section 1101 instructed the HHS Secretary to establish a temporary program— PCIP—to provide health insurance coverage for eligible individuals who have been uninsured for six months

Table 1. (Continued)

Summary of Administrative Action	Explanatory Notes and Comments
April 30, 2014, at which time the program would be terminated. [Note: The PCIP program was originally scheduled to terminate on January 1, 2014. However, on December 12, 2013, HHS announced that the PCIP program would be extended through the end of January 2014. Then on January 14, 2014, HHS announced that individuals could keep their PCIP coverage for two additional months, through March 31, 2014.] HHS provided former PCIP participants with a 60-day special enrollment period, beginning on May 1, 2014, to enroll in a QHP offered through an exchange. The new coverage is effective back to May 1 to avoid a lapse in health insurance coverage.	and have a pre-existing condition. PCIP was federally administered in 23 states and DC; the remaining states administered their own PCIPs. The ACA appropriated $5 billion, to remain available without fiscal year limitation, to pay claims against (and administrative costs of) PCIPs that are in excess of premiums collected from enrollees. The federally-run PCIP and state-run PCIPs stopped accepting new enrollees on February 16, 2013, and March 2, 2013, respectively, because of the finite amount of available funding. Under the law, PCIP coverage was to end on January 1, 2014, and the Secretary was instructed to develop procedures for transitioning individuals enrolled in PCIP into qualified health plans offered through the exchanges. However, ACA Section 1101(g)(3) gave the Secretary the authority to extend PCIP coverage, if necessary, to avoid a lapse in coverage for such individuals. For more information, see https://www.pcip.gov/.
Basic Health Plan Option	
On February 7, 2013, HHS announced that implementation of the Basic Health Program (BHP) would be delayed by one year until 2015. The BHP gives states the option of using ACA subsidies to help cover certain low-income individuals whose income is too high to qualify for Medicaid. See http://www.medicaid.gov/StateResource-Center/FAQ-Medicaid-and-CHIP-Affordable-Care-Act-Implementation/Downloads/FAQs-by-Topic-BHP.pdf.	ACA Section 1331, as amended, permits states to establish a BHP in which states contract with private-sector and cooperative health plans to provide health insurance coverage for certain low-income individuals not eligible for the state's Medicaid program with incomes between 133% and 200% of the federal poverty level. States that decide to offer a BHP receive federal funding equal to 95% of the value of the premium tax credits and cost-sharing subsidies that eligible individuals would have received had they purchased coverage through an exchange. For more information, see http://medicaid.gov/Basic-Health-Program/Behavioral-Health-Program.html.
Small Business Health Options Program (SHOP) Exchanges	

Summary of Administrative Action	Explanatory Notes and Comments
HHS's June 4, 2013, final rule for the SHOP exchanges included a transition policy that delayed until 2015 the implementation of employee choice in federally facilitated SHOP exchanges. For plan years beginning in 2014, federally facilitated SHOP exchanges will only allow employers to select one QHP to offer to their employees, while state-based SHOP exchanges may allow employers to choose one or more QHPs to offer to their employees. See 78 *Federal Register* 33233, http://www.gpo.gov/ fdsys/pkg/FR-2013-06-04/pdf/2013-13149.pdf. HHS's May 27, 2014, final rule on exchange and market standards for 2015 gives state insurance commissioners the option to recommend that a SHOP exchange delay implementation of employee choice until 2016. See 79 *Federal Register* 30239, http://www.gpo.gov/fdsys/ pkg/FR2014-05-27/pdf/2014-11657.pdf.	ACA Section 1311 requires each state (or the federal government on its behalf) to establish a SHOP exchange through which small employers will be able to purchase plans for their employees. Initially, states can choose to open SHOP exchanges to companies with up to 100 employees or limit participation to companies with 50 or fewer employees. By 2016, states must open the exchanges to companies with up to 100 employees. Beginning in 2017, states have the option to open SHOP exchanges to companies with more than 100 employees. Employers with fewer than 25 employees may qualify for tax credits if they purchase insurance coverage for their employees through a SHOP exchange. For more information, see https://www.healthcare.gov/ small-businesses/.
On November 27, 2013, HHS announced that federally facilitated SHOP exchanges will not accept online enrollments for one year, until November 2014. In the meantime, small businesses can enroll in plans listed on these exchanges through an insurance agent or broker, or directly with the insurance carrier. [Note: This announcement represented the third delay in launching the online SHOP exchange, which was originally expected to be fully functional at the beginning of October 2013.] See http://www.hhs.gov/ healthcare/facts/blog/2013/11/direct-new-path-to-shopmarketplace.html. On March 14, 2014, CMS announced that it would consider requests from states that are not yet able to enroll small businesses through their SHOP exchanges online to use the same direct enrollment approach that the federally facilitated SHOP exchanges have implemented for 2014. See http://www.cms.gov/ CCIIO/Resources/Fact-Sheets-and-FAQs/Downloads/retroactive-	Employee choice refers to giving employees the option to choose from more than one QHP offered by an employer. Under this policy, an employer picks a level of coverage based on actuarial value (i.e., the bronze, silver, gold, or platinum tier) and the employees can then choose any plan offered within that tier of coverage. Eighteen states with a federally facilitated SHOP exchange have elected to delay employee choice until 2016. The remaining 14 states with a federally facilitated SHOP exchange will join most state-based SHOP exchanges in making employee choice available in 2015. See http://www.cms.gov/CCIIO/Programs-and-Initiatives/HealthInsurance-Marketplaces/2015-Transition-to-Employee-Choice-.html.

Table 1. (Continued)

Summary of Administrative Action	Explanatory Notes and Comments
advance-paymentsptc-csrs-03-14-14.pdf.	
Electronic Reporting	
HHS's July 15, 2013, final rule on health insurance exchange eligibility and enrollment delayed until 2015 a requirement that state Medicaid agencies provide notices electronically to beneficiaries. Between October 1, 2013, and January 1, 2015, state Medicaid agencies must give individuals the choice to receive notices in electronic format or by regular mail. Agencies must ensure that an individual's choice to receive electronic notices is confirmed by regular mail, and must inform the individual of his or her right to switch to receiving notice through regular mail. [42 C.F.R. 435.918] See 78 *Federal Register* 42159, http://www.gpo.gov/fdsys /pkg/FR-2013-07-15/pdf/2013- 16271.pdf.	Exchanges must also provide required notices by regular mail or, if an individual elects, electronically, provided that the specifications for electronic notices in 42 C.F.R. 435.918 are met. However, exchanges may choose to delay until 2015 the requirement in 42 C.F.R. 435.918(b)(1) that individuals who elect to receive electronic notices receive confirmation by mail. [45 C.F.R. 155.230(d)]

Source: Prepared by the Congressional Research Service based on a review of the documents cited in the table.

End Notes

[1] The ACA was signed into law on March 23, 2010 (P.L. 111-148). On March 30, 2010, the President signed the Health Care and Education Reconciliation Act (HCERA; P.L. 111-152), which amended numerous provisions in the ACA. HCERA also included multiple new freestanding provisions related to the ACA. Several other bills enacted during the 111th and 112th Congresses made additional changes to selected ACA provisions. All references to the ACA in this report refer, collectively, to the law as amended and to the related HCERA provisions.

[2] CRS Report R43289, Legislative Actions to Repeal, Defund, or Delay the Affordable Care Act, by C. Stephen Redhead and Janet Kinzer.

[3] A detailed examination of the ACA is beyond the scope of this report. Readers who are unfamiliar with the ACA's provisions to restructure the private health insurance market and expand access to affordable health insurance through the competitive marketplaces—or exchanges—and the expansion of state Medicaid programs will find numerous CRS products that provide more in-depth information on the law at http://www.crs.gov/ pages/subissue.aspx?cliid=3746& parentid=13&preview=False.

[4] Internal Revenue Service, "Transition Relief for 2014 Under §§ 6055 (Information Reporting), 6056 (Information Reporting) and 4980H (Employer Shared Responsibility Provisions)," Notice 2013-45, July 9, 2013, http://www.irs.gov/pub/irs-drop/n-13-45.PDF.

[5] The White House, "Fact Sheet: New Administration Proposal to Help Consumers Facing Cancellations," November 14, 2013, http://www.whitehouse.gov/the-press-office/2013/11/14/fact-sheet-new-administration-proposal-helpconsumers-facing-cancellatio.

[6] Department of Health & Human Services, Centers for Medicare & Medicaid Services, "Insurance Standards Bulletin Series - Extension of Transitional Policy through October 1, 2016," March 5, 2014, http://www.cms.gov/CCIIO/ Resources/Regulations-and-Guidance/Downloads/transition-to-compliant-policies-03-06-2015.pdf.

[7] Department of Health & Human Services, Centers for Medicare & Medicaid Services, "Guidance for Issuers on Special Enrollment Periods for Complex Cases in the Federally-facilitated Marketplace after the Initial Open Enrollment Period," March 26, 2014, http://www.cms.gov/CCIIO/Resources/Regulations-and-Guidance/Downloads/ complex-cases-SEP-3-26-2014.pdf.

[8] Simon Lazarus, "Delaying Parts of Obamacare: 'Blatantly Illegal' or Routine Adjustment?," The Atlantic, July 17, 2013, http://www.theatlantic.com/national/archive/2013/07/delaying-parts-of-obamacare-blatantly-illegal-or-routineadjustment/277873/.

[9] Timothy Stoltzfus Jost and Simon Lazarus, "Obama's ACA Delays - Breaking the Law or Making it Work?," New England Journal of Medicine, April 2, 2014, http://www.nejm.org/doi/pdf/10.1056/NEJMp1403294.

[10] Section 7805(a) of the Internal Revenue Code; 26 U.S.C. §7805(a).

[11] Letter from Mark J. Mazur, Assistant Secretary for Tax Policy, to Honorable Fred Upton, Chairman, Committee on Energy and Commerce, July 9, 2013, http://democrats.energycommerce.house.gov/sites/default/files/documents/UptonTreasury-ACA-2013-7-9.pdf. For a legal analysis of the Administration's decision to delay enforcement of the employer mandate, see CRS Legal Sidebar, Obama Administration Delays Implementation of ACA's Employer Responsibility Requirements: A Brief Legal Overview, posted July 8, 2013, http://www.crs.gov/LegalSidebar/ details.aspx?ProdId=582.

[12] Nicholas Bagley, "The Legality of Delaying Key Elements of the ACA," New England Journal of Medicine, April 2, 2014, http://www.nejm.org/doi/pdf/10.1056/NEJMp1402641. For a legal analysis of the Administration's decision to permit insurers to renew noncompliant policies for individuals and small businesses, see CRS Legal Sidebar, Obama Administration's "Fix" for Insurance Cancellations: A Legal Overview, posted November 18, 2013, http://www.crs.gov/LegalSidebar/details.aspx?ProdId=724.

[13] Full text of the resolution is at http://www.gpo.gov/fdsys/pkg/BILLS-113hres676rh/pdf/BILLS-113hres676rh.pdf. H.Res. 676 is a simple resolution; that is, a non-legislative measure that is effective only in the chamber in which it was approved. It does not require concurrence by the other chamber (Senate) or approval by the President.

[14] Jonathan Weisman, "Suit Against Obama to Focus on Health Law, Boehner Says," New York Times, July 10, 2014, http://www.nytimes.com/2014/07/11/us/politics/boehner-says-obama-lawsuit-will-focus-on-health-law.html?ref=us& r=0.

In: Delay and Discretion …
Editor: Cory Derricks

ISBN: 978-1-63463-482-3

Chapter 5

Prosecutorial Discretion in Immigration Enforcement: Legal Issues*

Kate M. Manuel and Todd Garvey

Summary

The term *prosecutorial discretion* is commonly used to describe the wide latitude that prosecutors have in determining when, whom, how, and even whether to prosecute apparent violations of the law. The Immigration and Naturalization Service (INS) and, later, the Department of Homeland Security (DHS) and its components have historically described themselves as exercising prosecutorial discretion in immigration enforcement. Some commentators have recently challenged this characterization on the grounds that DHS enforces primarily civil violations, and some of its components cannot be said to engage in "law enforcement," as that term is conventionally understood. However, even agencies that do not prosecute or engage in law enforcement have been recognized as having discretion (sometimes referred to as *enforcement discretion*) in determining whether to enforce particular violations.

Federal regulation of immigration is commonly said to arise from various powers enumerated in the Constitution (e.g., naturalization,

* This is an edited, reformatted and augmented version of a Congressional Research Service publication R42924, prepared for Members and Committees of Congress dated December 27, 2013.

commerce), as well as the federal government's inherent power to control and conduct foreign relations. Some, although not all, of these powers belong exclusively to Congress, and courts have sometimes described Congress as having "plenary power" over immigration. However, few courts or commentators have addressed the separation of powers between Congress and the President in the field of immigration, and the executive has sometimes been said to share plenary power over immigration with Congress as one of the "political branches." Moreover, the authority to exercise prosecutorial or enforcement discretion has traditionally been understood to arise from the Constitution, not from any congressional delegation of power.

Certain decisions have been widely recognized as within the prosecutorial discretion of immigration officers. These include deciding whether to initiate removal proceedings and what charges to lodge against the respondent; canceling a Notice to Appear or other charging document before jurisdiction vests with an immigration judge; granting deferred action or extended voluntary departure to an alien otherwise subject to removal (deportation); appealing particular decisions or orders; and imposing fines for particular offenses, among other things. Enforcement priorities and resources, as well as humanitarian concerns, have typically played a role in determining whether to exercise discretion in individual cases. For example, the George W. Bush Administration temporarily suspended employer sanctions in areas affected by Hurricane Katrina, and the Obama Administration recently began granting deferred action to certain unauthorized aliens brought to the United States as children.

While the executive branch's prosecutorial or enforcement discretion is broad, it is not unfettered, and particular exercises of discretion could potentially be checked by the Constitution, statute, or agency directives. *Selective prosecution*, or prosecution based on race, religion, or the exercise of constitutional rights, is prohibited, although aliens generally cannot assert selective prosecution as a defense to removal. A policy of non-enforcement that amounts to an abdication of an agency's statutory responsibilities could potentially be said to violate the Take Care Clause. However, standing to challenge alleged violations of the Take Care Clause may be limited, and no court appears to have invalidated a policy of non-enforcement founded upon prosecutorial discretion on the grounds that the policy violated the Take Care Clause. Non-enforcement of particular laws could also potentially be challenged under the Administrative Procedure Act if a statute provides specific guidelines for the agency to follow in exercising its enforcement powers. In addition, an agency could potentially be found to have constrained its own discretion, as some courts found that the INS had done in the 1970s with its operating instruction on deferred action.

Introduction

The term *prosecutorial discretion* is commonly used to describe the "wide latitude" that prosecutors have in determining when, whom, how, and even whether to prosecute apparent violations of the law.[1] The Immigration and Naturalization Service (INS) and, later, the Department of Homeland Security (DHS) and its components have historically described themselves as exercising prosecutorial discretion in the enforcement of federal immigration law, which is largely contained in the Immigration and Nationality Act of 1952 (INA), as amended.[2] Some commentators have recently challenged this characterization on the grounds that DHS enforces primarily civil violations, and some of its components cannot be said to engage in "law enforcement," as that term is conventionally understood.[3] However, even agencies that do not prosecute or engage in law enforcement have been recognized as having discretion (sometimes referred to as *enforcement discretion*) in determining whether to enforce particular violations,[4] and immigration officers appear to have exercised such discretion in individual cases and on a categorical basis for decades. For example, the Kennedy Administration granted extended voluntary departure to persons from Cuba in 1960,[5] allowing many otherwise deportable Cuban nationals to remain in the United States for an extended period, while the George W. Bush Administration temporarily suspended employer sanctions on entities that employed unauthorized aliens in areas affected by Hurricane Katrina.[6]

The scope of prosecutorial discretion in immigration enforcement has recently been of interest to Congress and the public due to certain initiatives of the Obama Administration.[7] In 2011, John Morton, then Director of U.S. Customs and Immigration Enforcement (ICE), issued two memoranda addressing prosecutorial discretion, one of which identified ICE's priorities for the apprehension, detention, and removal of aliens,[8] and the other of which discussed how ICE personnel may exercise prosecutorial discretion consistent with ICE's enforcement priorities.[9] Subsequently, in June 2012, then Secretary of Homeland Security Janet Napolitano issued a memorandum "setting forth how, in the exercise of [its] prosecutorial discretion, the Department ... should enforce the Nation's immigration laws against certain young people who were brought to this country as children and know only this country as home."[10] As implemented, this initiative has come to be known as Deferred Action for Childhood Arrivals (DACA). Most recently, ICE has directed its personnel to exercise discretion in "ensur[ing] that the agency's immigration enforcement activities do not unnecessarily disrupt the parental rights of both alien parents or legal guardians of minor children."[11]

These initiatives have been challenged by some Members of Congress and commentators on the grounds that they are tantamount to "amnesty" for unauthorized aliens and are contrary to the President's constitutional responsibility to "take Care" that the laws be enforced.[12] In particular, some Members have suggested that DACA exceeds the President's authority because "it was issued after Congress specifically rejected legislation"—the Development, Relief, and Education for Alien Minors (DREAM) Act—"embodying that policy."[13] In addition, several ICE agents and the State of Mississippi filed suit in federal district court for the Northern District of Texas alleging that the DACA initiative violates certain statutory requirements and impinges upon Congress's legislative powers, among other things.[14]

This report begins by discussing the sources of federal power to regulate immigration and, particularly, the allocation of power between Congress and the President in this area. It next addresses the constitutional and other foundations for the doctrine of prosecutorial discretion, as well as the potential ways in which prosecutorial discretion may be exercised in the immigration context. It concludes by addressing potential constitutional, statutory, and administrative constraints upon the exercise of prosecutorial discretion. The report does not address other aspects of discretion in immigration law, such as the discretion exercised by immigration officers in granting benefits (e.g., asylum), or by immigration judges in non-enforcement contexts (e.g., cancellation of removal).[15]

FEDERAL POWER TO REGULATE IMMIGRATION

The Constitution does not directly address the sources of federal power to regulate which nonU.S. nationals (aliens) may enter and remain in the United States, or to establish the conditions of their continued presence within the country. However, several of the enumerated powers of the federal government have been construed as authorizing such regulation. The powers to establish a uniform rule of naturalization and regulate commerce are arguably the most commonly cited provisions, particularly in recent years.[16] Various authorities related to foreign affairs have also been routinely cited as providing support for particular enactments and activities in the field of immigration.[17] In addition, in some cases, the Supreme Court has suggested that federal regulation of immigration is grounded in the federal government's "inherent power as a sovereign to control and conduct foreign relations."[18]

Many, although not all, of these powers belong exclusively to Congress,[19] and courts and commentators have sometimes used language which implies that Congress is preeminent in the field of immigration. For example, it has frequently been said that Congress has "plenary power" over immigration,[20] and that "over no conceivable subject is the legislative power of Congress more complete than it is over" immigration.[21] In some cases, courts have even suggested that the executive branch's authority over immigration arises from a delegation of congressional power, as is the case with other Article I powers, although Article I does not give Congress clear supremacy over immigration, as previously noted.[22] In *Sale v. Haitian Centers Council, Inc.*, for example, the Supreme Court rejected a challenge which alleged that the executive branch's procedures for screening Haitian migrants at sea, without allowing them to disembark in the United States, did not comply with statutory and treaty-based protections that enable aliens to apply for refugee status and avoid repatriation.[23] The Court did so, in part, on the grounds that "[t]he laws that the Coast Guard is engaged in enforcing when it takes to the seas under orders to prevent aliens from illegally crossing our borders are laws whose administration has been assigned to the Attorney General by Congress."[24] Similarly, in other cases, the Court has described Congress's power to exclude aliens from the United States, or prescribe the terms and conditions upon which they may enter, as being "enforced exclusively through executive officers,"[25] or opined that executive branch officials "exercise[] delegated legislative power" in taking specific actions.[26]

Few courts or commentators have, however, directly addressed the separation of powers between Congress and the President in the field of immigration,[27] and in some cases, the Court has also suggested that the executive branch shares plenary power over immigration with Congress as one of the "political branches."[28] While some such cases could potentially be construed as referring to powers delegated to the executive branch by Congress, in other cases, the President has been expressly said to have inherent authority over at least some immigration-related matters. For example, in *United States ex rel. Knauff v. Shaughnessy*, the Court upheld the executive branch's decision to exclude a German "war bride," in part, on the grounds that

> The exclusion of aliens is a fundamental act of sovereignty. The right to do so stems not alone from legislative power but is inherent in the

> executive power to control the foreign affairs of the nation.... When Congress prescribes a procedure concerning the admissibility of aliens, it is not dealing alone with a legislative power. It is implementing an inherent executive power.[29]

Similarly, in *Hampton v. Mow Sung Wong*, the Court indicated that certain rules adopted by the U.S. Civil Service Commission barring resident aliens from employment in the federal civil service impermissibly deprived these aliens of due process of law, but that such rules would be permissible if they "were expressly mandated by the Congress or the President."[30] Here, Congress had delegated authority to the President to prescribe regulations for the admission of individuals to the civil service. Accordingly, it is possible that when the *Hampton* Court referred to the President's power to limit alien eligibility for federal employment, it intended to refer only to the power which had been conferred to him by Congress. On the other hand, the Court's discussion of the interests of the President that might be sufficient to justify the exclusion of noncitizens from the civil service focused upon the President's power to negotiate treaties, suggesting recognition of some independent constitutional basis for executive branch activity in the field of immigration.[31]

The possibility of independent executive branch authority over immigration is significant in that any such authority could potentially help justify certain actions taken by the executive branch (although actions taken in reliance on such authority could also potentially raise issues if they were arguably within Congress's purview).[32] However, the executive branch's authority to exercise prosecutorial or enforcement discretion has traditionally been understood to arise from the Constitution,[33] as discussed below.

Courts have historically not required that the executive branch have specific statutory authorization for particular exercises of prosecutorial discretion. Thus, immigration officials would not necessarily be precluded from granting deferred action, or taking certain other actions that could permit otherwise removable aliens to remain in the United States, just because federal immigration statutes do not expressly authorize such actions.[34] On the other hand, Section 103(a)(3) of the INA authorizes the Secretary of Homeland Security to "perform such other acts as he deems necessary for carrying out his authority under the provisions of this chapter," and has been construed by some as "commit[ting] enforcement of the INA to [the Secretary's] discretion."[35] The federal government recently noted its discretion under Section 103(a)(3) in seeking dismissal of a lawsuit challenging the DACA initiative.[36] The Secretary's authority under Section 103(a)(3) of the INA is, however, an authority granted to the executive branch by Congress and, as such, is distinguishable from the President's constitutional authority to "take Care" that the laws be enforced. Congress could, for example, potentially limit the discretion granted to the Secretary by Section 103(a)(3) of the INA, including by prohibiting particular exercises of discretion. In contrast, Congress probably could not directly limit the President's authority under the Constitution to "take Care" that the laws be enforced.

The INA also grants the Secretary other types of discretion which are sometimes mentioned in connection with exercises of prosecutorial or enforcement discretion, but do not themselves involve determinations regarding when, whom, how, and even whether to prosecute apparent violations of the law. In some cases, the INA expressly provides that certain determinations are within the discretion of immigration officials, such as the determination to waive the bar upon admissibility for alien spouses or children of U.S. citizens or lawful permanent residents (LPRs) who have been present in the United States without authorization for more than 180 days.[37] In other cases, the INA does not expressly mention the discretion of executive branch officials, but effectively affords them such discretion by leaving certain details of the statutory scheme to be implemented by the executive branch. Thus, the INA affords the Secretary discretion to determine which aliens are granted employment authorization by prohibiting the employment of unauthorized aliens, and defining "unauthorized alien," in part, as an alien who has not been "authorized to be ... employed by the [Secretary]."[38] Because it is conferred by Congress, this discretion, like the Secretary's discretion under Section 103(a)(3), could also be limited by Congress.

PROSECUTORIAL DISCRETION GENERALLY

The judicial branch has traditionally accorded federal prosecutors "broad" latitude in making a range of investigatory and prosecutorial determinations, including when, whom, and whether to prosecute particular violations of federal law.[39] This doctrine of "prosecutorial discretion" has a long historical pedigree—the early roots of which can be traced at least to a Sixteenth Century English common law procedural mechanism known as the *nolle prosequi*.[40] In the early English legal system, criminal prosecutions were generally initiated by private individuals rather than public prosecutors. The *nolle prosequi*, however, allowed the government, generally at the direction of the Crown, to intervene in and terminate a privately initiated criminal action it viewed as "frivolous or in contravention of royal interests."[41] The discretionary device was later adopted into American common law and has been used by prosecutors to terminate criminal prosecutions that are determined to be unwarranted or which the prosecuting authority chooses not to pursue.[42]

Notwithstanding this historical background, the modern doctrine of prosecutorial discretion derives more from our constitutional structure than English common law. However, the exact justification for the doctrine does not appear to have been explicitly established. Generally, courts have characterized prosecutorial discretion as a function of some mixture of the separation of powers, the Take Care Clause,[43] or the duties of a prosecutor as an appointee of the President.[44] Moreover, both federal and state courts have ruled that the exercise of prosecutorial discretion is an executive function necessary to the proper administration of justice. Given these precedents, prosecutorial discretion may be appropriately characterized as a constitutionally based doctrine.

Regardless of its precise textual source, courts generally will neither review nor question discretionary prosecutorial decisions, nor "coerce" the executive branch to initiate a particular prosecution. In acknowledging the discretion possessed by enforcement officials, courts have recognized that the "decision to prosecute is particularly ill-suited to judicial review," as it involves the consideration of factors—such as the strength of evidence, deterrence value, and existing enforcement priorities—"not readily susceptible to the kind of analysis the courts are competent to undertake."[45] Moreover, the executive branch has asserted that "because the essential core of the President's constitutional responsibility is the duty to enforce the laws, the Executive Branch has *exclusive* authority to initiate and prosecute actions to enforce the laws adopted by Congress."[46]

An agency decision to initiate an enforcement action in the *administrative* context "shares to some extent the characteristics of the decision of a prosecutor in the executive branch" to initiate a prosecution in the *criminal* context.[47] Thus, just as courts are hesitant to question a prosecutor's decisions with respect to whether to bring a criminal prosecution, so too are courts cautious in reviewing an agency's decision not to bring an enforcement action. In the seminal case of *Heckler v. Cheney*, the Supreme Court held that "an agency's decision not to prosecute or enforce, whether through civil or criminal process, is a decision generally committed to an agency's absolute discretion."[48] The Court noted that agency enforcement decisions, like prosecution decisions, involve a "complicated balancing" of agency interests and resources—a balancing that the agency is "better equipped" to evaluate than the courts.[49] The *Heckler* opinion proceeded to establish the standard for the reviewability of agency non-enforcement decisions, holding that an "agency's decision not to take enforcement action should be presumed immune from judicial review."[50] However, the Court indicated that, in certain cases, that presumption may be overcome "where the substantive statute has provided guidelines for the agency to follow in exercising its enforcement powers," [51] as is discussed below.

PROSECUTORIAL DISCRETION IN THE IMMIGRATION CONTEXT

In *Reno v. American-Arab Anti-Discrimination Committee*, a majority of the Supreme Court found that the various prudential concerns that prompt deference to the executive branch's determinations as to whether to prosecute criminal offenses are "greatly magnified in the deportation context,"[52] which entails civil (rather than criminal) proceedings.[53] While the reasons cited by the Court for greater deference to exercises of prosecutorial discretion in the immigration context than in other contexts reflect the facts of the case, which arose when certain removable aliens challenged the government's decision *not* to exercise prosecutorial discretion in their favor,[54] the Court's language is broad and arguably can be construed to encompass decisions to favorably exercise such discretion. More recently, in its decision in *Arizona v. United States*, a majority of the Court arguably similarly affirmed the authority of the executive branch not to seek the removal of certain aliens, noting that "[a] principal feature of the removal system is the broad discretion entrusted to immigration officials," and that "[r]eturning an alien to his own country may be deemed inappropriate even where he has committed a removable offense or fails to meet the criteria for admission."[55] According to the majority, such exercises of prosecutorial discretion may reflect "immediate human concerns" and the "equities of ... individual case[s]," such as whether the alien has children born in the United States or ties to the community, as well as "policy choices that bear on ... international relations."[56]

Going beyond such general affirmations of the executive branch's prosecutorial discretion in the immigration context, other cases have specifically noted that certain decisions are within the prosecutorial discretion of INS and, later, the immigration components of DHS. These decisions include

- whether to parole an alien into the United States;[57]
- whether to commence removal proceedings and what charges to lodge against the respondent;[58]
- whether to pursue formal removal proceedings;[59]
- whether to cancel a Notice to Appear or other charging document before jurisdiction vests with an immigration judge;[60]
- whether to grant deferred action or extended voluntary departure;[61]
- whether to appeal an immigration judge's decision or order, and whether to file a motion to reopen;[62]
- whether to invoke an automatic stay during the pendency of an appeal;[63] and
- whether to impose a fine for particular offenses.[64]

As used here, *deferred action* is "generally an act of prosecutorial discretion to suspend [taking action] against a particular individual or group of individuals for a specific timeframe; it cannot resolve an individual's underlying immigration status."[65] It is generally granted on a case-by-case basis, although the executive branch has sometimes provided that individuals who share certain characteristics (e.g., advanced or young age) are to be given particular consideration for deferred action.[66] In contrast, *extended voluntary departure*—sometimes also referred to as *deferred departure* or *deferred enforced departure*—generally involves "blanket relief" from removal to particular countries.[67]

Many of the actions that judicial and administrative tribunals have noted are within the prosecutorial discretion of immigration officers have also been mentioned in INS and, later, DHS, guidance regarding the exercise of prosecutorial discretion. Memoranda or other documents providing such guidance have been issued intermittently since at least 1976, and have suggested that officers may generally exercise discretion in

- deciding whether to issue or cancel a notice of detainer;
- deciding whether to issue, reissue, serve, file, or cancel a Notice to Appear;
- focusing administrative resources on particular violations or conduct;
- deciding whom to stop, question, or arrest for a violation;
- deciding whether to detain aliens who are not subject to "mandatory detention" pending removal, or whether to release them on bond, supervision, personal recognizance, or other conditions;
- seeking expedited removal or removal by means other than formal proceedings in immigration court;
- settling or dismissing a proceeding;
- granting deferred action or parole;
- staying a final order of removal;
- agreeing to voluntary departure, the withdrawal of an application for admission, or other action in lieu of a formal order of removal;
- pursuing an appeal;
- executing a removal order; and
- responding to or joining in a motion to reopen removal proceedings, or joining in a motion to grant relief or a benefit.[68]

Often, this executive branch guidance has highlighted resource constraints,[69] as well as humanitarian considerations,[70] that may warrant a favorable exercise of prosecutorial discretion, although such guidance has generally also indicated that determinations as to whether to exercise discretion in particular cases are to be based on the "totality of the circumstances"[71] and whether a "substantial federal interest" is present.[72] The guidance may also suggest when in the process such discretion is to be exercised (generally as early in the process as possible, so as to avoid wasting government resources),[73] as well as which officers may exercise particular forms of discretion.[74] While personnel are generally instructed that they should "always consider prosecutorial discretion on a case-by-case basis,"[75] classes of individuals warranting consideration for favorable—or unfavorable—exercises of discretion have sometimes been identified (e.g., minors and elderly individuals, known gang members).[76]

POTENTIAL LIMITS ON THE EXERCISE OF DISCRETION

While prosecutorial discretion is broad, it is not "unfettered,"[77] and particular exercises of discretion could potentially be checked by the Constitution, statute, or agency directives.[78] In practice, however, persons who are neither aliens nor otherwise subject to the requirements of the INA could lack standing to challenge alleged abuses of prosecutorial discretion in the immigration context. Standing is generally limited to persons who allege a "personal injury fairly traceable to the defendant's allegedly unlawful conduct and likely to be redressed by the requested relief."[79] Those whose sole injury is the government's alleged failure to follow the law will generally be found to lack standing because this injury is not personal and particularized.[80] Even government officers and employees, who have taken an oath to uphold the law, will generally be found to lack standing so long as their only asserted injury is being forced to violate their oaths by implementing an allegedly unlawful policy or practice.[81] Instead, they must allege some separate and concrete adverse consequence that would flow from violating their oath, and courts have reached differing conclusions as to whether the possibility of being disciplined for obeying—or refusing to obey—allegedly unlawful orders suffices for purposes of standing, or whether such injury is "entirely speculative."[82] Courts have imposed these limitations, in part, on the grounds that recognizing standing in such cases would allow persons to sue "merely ... to ensure [that federal] law conforms to [their] *opinion* of what federal law requires," and such personal opinions could change at any time.[83]

In addition, even where standing to challenge particular exercises of prosecutorial discretion exists, plaintiffs could potentially have difficulty obtaining relief given that actions by Congress or the President in the immigration context are generally subject to a "narrow standard of review,"[84] particularly in cases where such decisions implicate foreign affairs or national security. For example, in its recent decision in *Arizona v. United States*, a majority of the Supreme Court noted that "[s]ome discretionary decisions involve policy choices that bear on this Nation's international relations" when explaining the basis for the "broad discretion" immigration officers have in determining whether to remove unauthorized aliens.[85] The Court has similarly emphasized the potential "diplomatic repercussions" of certain decisions made by immigration officers (e.g., determining whether to grant withholding of removal or an alien's petition to reopen deportation proceedings).[86] Moreover, in some cases, courts have found that challenges to the alleged nonenforcement of immigration laws involve nonjusticiable political questions because they fundamentally entail disagreements about the proper extent of immigration enforcement.[87]

Constitution

The U.S. Constitution can be seen as imposing two potential limitations upon the executive branch's exercise of prosecutorial discretion, one in cases where the Executive decides to enforce the law against particular individuals because of their race, religion, exercise of a constitutional right, or other impermissible factors; and the other in cases where the Executive adopts a general policy of non-enforcement "which is in effect an abdication of its statutory duty."[88]

Selective Prosecution

In discussing the scope of the executive branch's prosecutorial discretion, courts have repeatedly noted that the determination as to whether to prosecute may not be "deliberately based upon an unjustifiable standard such as race, religion, or other arbitrary classification,"[89] including the exercise of protected statutory and constitutional rights.[90] Prosecutions (or other enforcement actions) that are based upon these factors could potentially be found to be impermissible, as was the case in *Yick Wo v. Hopkins*. There, the Supreme Court found that prosecutors' practice of enforcing a state law prohibiting the operation of laundries against only persons of Chinese descent ran afoul of the Equal Protection Clause.[91] In practice, however, defendants generally find it difficult to maintain a claim of selective prosecution because of the executive branch's prosecutorial discretion. Because such claims are seen as "invad[ing] a special province of the Executive," courts generally require defendants to introduce "clear evidence" displacing the presumption that the prosecutor has acted lawfully.[92] Specifically, they must show that (1) they were singled out for prosecution on an impermissible basis; (2) the government had a policy of declining to prosecute similarly situated defendants of other races, religions, etc.; and (3) the policy was motivated by a discriminatory purpose.[93]

Claims of selective prosecution can be even more difficult to maintain in an immigration context because the various prudential concerns that prompt deference to the executive branch's determinations as to whether to prosecute particular criminal offenses are "greatly magnified in the deportation context."[94] In fact, in *Reno v. American-Arab Anti-Discrimination Committee*, discussed above, the Supreme Court effectively foreclosed many claims of selective prosecution in removal proceedings by finding that "[a]s a general matter ... an alien unlawfully in this country has no constitutional right to assert selective enforcement as a defense against his deportation."[95] The petitioners in *Reno* had alleged that they were targeted for deportation because of the exercise of their First Amendment rights. All belonged to a group that the government characterized as an "international terrorist and communist organization," and they asserted that the INS did not enforce "routine status requirements," such as were enforced against them, against aliens who were not members of similarly disfavored groups.[96] However, a majority of the Court rejected the petitioners' arguments, in part, because it viewed "selective prosecution" as unusual even in the criminal context[97] and, in part, because it considered the exercise of prosecutorial discretion to be particularly significant in the immigration context, as previously noted. However, the *Reno* Court did leave open the possibility that a decision to remove an alien could potentially be struck down in a "rare case in which the alleged basis of discrimination is so outrageous that the foregoing considerations can be overcome,"[98] and subsequent cases continue to recognize the possibility of selective prosecution claims in the immigration context.[99]

"Take Care" Clause

Article II, Section 3 of the U.S. Constitution could also potentially constrain the executive branch's prosecutorial discretion in certain cases. When discussing the scope of such discretion, some courts have suggested that situations could potentially arise where the executive branch "expressly adopt[s] a general policy which is in effect an abdication of its statutory duty" by implementing a blanket ban on enforcement of a duly enacted statute.[100] In such situations, by refusing to enforce certain aspects of a statute, the executive branch could potentially be said to have exceeded the permissible scope of prosecutorial or enforcement discretion, and violated the President's duty that the "laws be faithfully executed."[101] However, no court appears to have invalidated a policy of non-enforcement founded upon prosecutorial discretion on the grounds that the policy violated the Take Care Clause, and one federal appellate court has opined that "[r]eal or perceived inadequate enforcement ... does not constitute a reviewable abdication of duty."[102] Rather, according to this court, to prove such an abdication, plaintiffs must show that the Executive either is "doing nothing to enforce the ... laws," or has "consciously decided to abdicate" its enforcement responsibilities.[103]

Some commentators have suggested that prosecutorial discretion policies which could result in the executive branch not enforcing the law against a large number of people constitute an abdication of statutory duty and, thus, violate the Take Care Clause.[104] This point has recently been made by some commentators with respect to the potentially 1.76 million individuals eligible to receive deferred action under DACA.[105] However, even if the INA were construed to impose a statutory duty to remove all unauthorized aliens, the fact that a large number of persons are favorably affected by a prosecutorial discretion policy might not, *per se*, suffice to prove a violation of the Take Care Clause. Courts might also consider the size of the total population against whom the law could be enforced, as well as the resources available for enforcing the law, on the theory that

> the President cannot secure full execution of the laws, if Congress denies to him adequate means of doing so. ... The President performs his full constitutional duty, if, with the means and instruments provided by Congress and within the limitations prescribed by it, he uses his best endeavors to secure the faithful execution of the laws enacted.[106]

Thus, in the case of DACA, for example, a reviewing court might note that DACA-eligible aliens represent a fraction of the estimated 11.5 million aliens who are present in the United States without authorization,[107] and ICE has the resources to remove annually less than 4% of the unauthorized alien population.[108]

The specific form of discretion exercised could also potentially play a role in a reviewing court's analysis of whether particular nonenforcement policies or practices constitute an abdication of a statutory duty. For example, a court could potentially distinguish between determinations to *delay enforcement actions* (e.g., granting deferred action or extended voluntary departure for a particular duration of time), and *determinations not to take enforcement actions* (e.g., determining whether to commence removal proceedings or cancel a notice for an alien to appear at removal proceedings), on the grounds that the Executive contemplates taking action in the future in the former cases.[109] Relatedly, a reviewing court might note whether the executive branch exercises its discretion on a case-by-case basis, taking into consideration the specific circumstances of the offense and the individual who committed it, or whether it has indicated its intention not to enforce particular offenses at all or against large groups of people. Such distinctions might, however, be difficult to draw with practices like the DACA initiative, in which exercises of discretion could be characterized as either individualized or categorical, depending upon how the initiative is viewed. DHS has repeatedly noted that determinations regarding whether to grant deferred action are to be made on a case-by-case basis for DACA-eligible individuals.[110] However, DHS has also established a broad category of individuals (e.g., those who came to the United States when they were under the age of 16, and are either currently in school or have graduated from high school) who are eligible to request deferred action pursuant to DACA.[111]

The existence of multiple—sometimes inconsistent—enforcement mandates from Congress might also factor into a court's analysis of whether particular nonenforcement policies or practices constitute an abdication of duty, particularly in situations where an agency elects to concentrate limited resources upon offenders (or offenses) that Congress has recently indicated are a priority. For example, following the enactment of the Illegal Immigration Reform and Immigrant Responsibility Act (IIRIRA), which some commentators assert amended the INA to require the removal of at least some unauthorized aliens, Congress enacted a number of measures directing DHS to give priority to the removal of "criminal aliens."[112] DHS has emphasized that its diminished focus on the removal of DACA-eligible individuals corresponds to an increased focus on criminal aliens,[113] and a reviewing court could potentially find that enforcement of later-enacted mandates (as to criminal aliens) may justify more limited enforcement of earlier enacted mandates (as to unauthorized aliens generally).

Statute

Another potential constraint upon the executive branch's exercise of prosecutorial discretion was noted by the Supreme Court in *Heckler v. Cheney*. There, the Court rejected a challenge to the Food and Drug Administration's (FDA's) decision not to exercise its enforcement authority over the use of certain drugs on the grounds that "an agency's decision not to take enforcement action should be presumed immune from judicial review under § 701(a)(2)" of the Administrative Procedure Act (APA).[114] Section 701(a)(2) of the APA generally bars review of "agency action [that] is committed to agency discretion by law,"[115] and the Court's statement here would suggest that it views exercises of prosecutorial discretion as generally committed to agency discretion by law. However, the *Heckler* Court also noted that this presumption of nonreviewability "may be rebutted where the substantive statute has provided guidelines for the agency to follow in exercising its enforcement powers.'"[116]

Determining whether a statute provides "guidelines" so as to make an agency's determination not to take enforcement action reviewable generally implicates questions of statutory interpretation. Such questions are not necessarily easily answered, though, as is illustrated by the argument that the executive branch lacks the discretion to grant deferred action to DACA beneficiaries because the INA requires the removal of aliens who entered the United States unlawfully.[117] This argument, which has recently been made by some commentators and litigants, rests upon three "interlocking provisions" in Section 235 of the INA that were added or amended by IIRIRA. Briefly summarized, these provisions state that

1. any alien present in the United States who has not been admitted shall be deemed an applicant for admission;
2. applicants for admission shall be inspected by immigration officers; and
3. in the case of an alien who is an applicant for admission, if the examining immigration officer determines that an alien seeking admission is not clearly and beyond a doubt entitled to be admitted, the alien shall be detained for removal proceedings.[118]

Those who view these provisions as requiring the removal of aliens who entered the United States unlawfully would appear to construe "shall" as indicating mandatory agency action, and all "applicants for admission" as "aliens seeking admission."

The federal district court reviewing ICE agents' challenge to the DACA initiative initially adopted this interpretation, finding that the INA's "use of the word 'shall' imposes a mandatory duty on immigration officers to initiate removal proceedings whenever they encounter 'applicants for admission' who are not 'clearly and beyond a doubt entitled to be admitted.'"[119] However, the court subsequently found that the same alleged injury that gave the plaintiffs standing to bring their challenge—namely, their "being compelled to violate a federal statute upon pain of adverse employment action"—means that their case is within the exclusive jurisdiction of the Merit Systems Protection Board (MSPB), and cannot be heard by a federal district court.[120]

No other court has addressed the construction of these three provisions of the INA as an "interlocking" whole. Another court, if it found that it had jurisdiction, could potentially adopt an alternate interpretation, particularly given prior decisions distinguishing between aliens within the United States who have not been admitted, and aliens seeking admission at ports of entry.[121] The Supreme Court's decision in *Arizona v. United States* could also potentially be said to support an alternate construction.[122] While the majority in *Arizona* did not directly address the DACA initiative, it expressly noted the "broad discretion exercised by immigration officials" in the removal process.[123] Because such discretion would arguably be inconsistent with a statutory requirement to place in removal proceedings all aliens who entered the United States unlawfully, the majority's decision suggests that the Court does not construe the INA as legally compelling immigration officers to place all aliens who entered the United States unlawfully in removal proceedings.

Courts could also potentially construe other provisions of the INA that use "shall" differently than the district court reviewing the ICE officers' challenge to DACA construed the three provisions noted above.

Whether "Shall" Means Agencies Lack Discretion

The argument that Section 235 of the INA requires that aliens who unlawfully entered the United States be placed in removal proceedings appears to rest on the use of "shall" in Section 235, and the view that "shall" indicates mandatory agency action. "Shall" frequently indicates required action, particularly when used in contexts that do not implicate an agency's enforcement discretion.[124] However, the use of "shall" in Section 235, or elsewhere in the INA, would not, in itself, necessarily be construed to mean that DHS is required to take particular actions, because courts have found that agencies may retain discretion even when a statute uses "shall."[125] The statute at issue in *Heckler*, for example, stated that

> [a]ny article of food, drug, or cosmetic that is adulterated or misbranded when introduced into or while in interstate commerce or while held for sale ... after shipment in interstate commerce, or which may not ... be introduced into interstate commerce, shall be liable to be proceeded against.[126]

Nonetheless, despite its use of "shall," this statutory provision was construed by the Court as "framed in the permissive."[127] The Board of Immigration Appeals (BIA), the highest administrative body for construing and applying immigration law, has also rejected the view that "shall" means that immigration officials necessarily lack discretion as to whether to take particular actions. For example, in a 2011 decision, the BIA found that determinations as to whether to pursue expedited removal proceedings under Section 235 of the INA or formal removal proceedings under Section 240 of the INA are within DHS's discretion, notwithstanding the fact that the INA uses "shall" in describing who is subject to expedited removal.[128] In so doing, the BIA specifically noted that

> in the Federal criminal code, Congress has defined most crimes by providing that whoever engages in certain conduct "shall" be imprisoned or otherwise punished. But this has never been construed to require a Federal prosecutor to bring charges against every person believed to have violated the statute.[129]

In light of these precedents, the use of "shall," in itself, might not suffice for a court to find that an agency lacks the discretion not to enforce particular statutory requirements against certain individuals. Rather, a reviewing court might also consider the overall "statutory scheme [and] its objectives."[130] For example, in *Dunlop v. Bachowski*, the Court found that the Department of Labor's alleged nonenforcement of a statute was reviewable, unlike with the statute at issue in *Heckler*. The statute in question used the word "shall," but the Court does not appear to have accorded any special significance to this word. Instead, the Court emphasized that the statute directed the Secretary of Labor to investigate certain complaints brought by members of labor organizations challenging the validity of union elections, and bring a civil action against the labor organization within 60 days of the complaint's filing if the Secretary finds probable cause to believe a violation occurred and has not been remedied.[131] Because of these provisions, the Court viewed the Secretary's discretion as limited to determining whether there is probable cause to believe that a violation occurred.[132] Similarly, in *Adams v. Richardson*, the U.S. Court of Appeals for the District of Columbia Circuit noted that the statute in question was not "so broad" as to preclude judicial review, since it "indicates with precision the measures available to enforce the Act."[133]

Deference to Agencies' Interpretations of Their Governing Statutes

Another potential issue that can arise in determining whether "shall" indicates mandatory agency action when used in particular statutory provisions is how the agency has construed the provision, and whether a court finds that the agency's interpretation is entitled to deference under the precedent of *Chevron, USA v. Natural Resources Defense Council.*[134] In *Chevron*, the

Supreme Court articulated a two-part test for review of an agency's construction of a statute which it administers: (1) Has Congress directly spoken to the precise question at issue? and (2) If not, is the agency's reasonable interpretation of the statute consistent with the purposes of the statute?[135] "[I]f the statute speaks clearly 'to the precise question at issue,'" the tribunal "must give effect to the unambiguously expressed intent of Congress,"[136] regardless of what the agency regulation provides. However, where "the statute is silent or ambiguous with respect to the specific issue," the tribunal "must sustain the [a]gency's interpretation if it is 'based on a permissible construction' of the Act."[137]

In the case of Section 235 of the INA, for example, the Department of Justice (DOJ) and, later, DHS have interpreted the relevant provisions of the INA in a somewhat different manner than those who argue that DHS lacks the discretion not to remove aliens who entered the United States unlawfully. Both DOJ/DHS and those who claim it lacks discretion construe the first two provisions of Section 235 of the INA noted above—aliens present without admission being deemed applicants for admission, and applicants for admission being inspected—as applying to both (1) "arriving aliens" at a port-of-entry and (2) aliens who are present in the United States without inspection. However, DOJ and DHS have differed from proponents of the view that DHS lacks discretion in that DOJ and DHS have construed the third provision—regarding detention of certain aliens seeking admission—as applicable only to arriving aliens, not aliens who are present without inspection.[138] This difference appears to have arisen, in part, because the agencies have emphasized the phrase "aliens seeking admission" in the third provision, and have reasoned that only arriving aliens at ports-of-entry can be said to be seeking admission.[139]

The district court reviewing ICE agents' challenge to the DACA initiative declined to grant any deference to DHS's interpretation here. The court found that this interpretation was not entitled to deference, in part, because it viewed the relevant provisions of the INA as unambiguously applying to both aliens coming (or attempting to come) into the United States at a port of entry, and aliens present in the United States without having been admitted.[140] It also found that DHS regulations did not support DHS's proposed interpretation because, while these regulations applied to arriving aliens, they were not limited to arriving aliens.[141] However, as previously noted, this court is the only court to have so reached this conclusion, and it subsequently found that it lacked jurisdiction over the ICE agents' claims.[142] It is unclear whether other courts would reach the same conclusion as to whether and how much deference should be accorded to DHS's interpretation of these three provisions of INA §235.

It should also be noted that the INS and, later, DHS have interpreted other provisions of the INA differently than §235, construing them as removing prosecutorial discretion as to certain determinations. For example, immigration authorities have long maintained that Section 236(c) of the INA—which states that immigration officials "shall take into custody" certain criminal aliens, and may release them only under narrow circumstances[143]—limits their discretion as to whether or not to release such aliens from custody.[144]

Executive Branch Self-Regulation

An agency could also potentially be found to have imposed certain constraints upon its exercise of prosecutorial discretion through either (1) the promulgation of regulations or (2) the issuance of guidelines that the agency intends to be binding or which have been employed in such a way as to be binding as a practical matter.[145] For example, in a 1979 decision, the U.S. Court of Appeals for the Ninth Circuit ("Ninth Circuit") found that an INS Operations Instruction addressing deferred action against deportable aliens was binding upon the agency because of its "purpose and effect."[146] In reaching this conclusion, the court emphasized that the Instruction more closely resembled a substantive provision for relief than an internal procedural guideline because it "exist[ed] out of consideration for the convenience of the petitioner, and not that of the INS."[147] The court further noted that the Instruction ostensibly required INS district directors to recommend deferred or "non-priority" status in certain cases, and that this status was periodically reviewed and not subject to termination at INS's convenience.[148] In short, the court distinguished the Instruction from other intra-agency guidelines that would create no substantive rights because the Instruction's effects were "final and permanent, with the same force as that of a Congressional statute."[149] Other courts reached different conclusions as to whether this particular Operations Instruction was binding,[150] and the INS subsequently amended to it to clarify that grants of deferred action were discretionary.[151] Later, the guideline was rescinded (although INS and, later, DHS continued to grant deferred action).[152] However, the 1979 case illustrates that certain types of "cabining of an agency's prosecutorial discretion" could potentially "rise to the level of a substantive, legislative rule" in the immigration context.[153] Were that the case, DHS's exercise of prosecutorial discretion could potentially be found to have been constrained by its own guidelines.

In its recent guidance regarding the exercise of prosecutorial discretion, DHS has consistently emphasized that "there is no right to a favorable exercise of prosecutorial discretion by the agency," and that nothing in the guidelines should be construed to prohibit the apprehension, detention, or removal of aliens unlawfully present in the United States, or to limit any legal authority to enforce federal immigration law.[154] However, an agency's characterization of its own policies as non-binding is not necessarily dispositive,[155] and certain parties challenging the DACA

initiative have suggested that, in "implementing the Directive, DHS has treated the Directive as if it were a rule."[156] No court appears to have addressed this argument, to date, but early in 2012— when DHS was conducting preliminary reviews of the dockets of the immigration courts in Baltimore and Denver for cases that might qualify for favorable exercises of prosecutorial discretion[157]—a panel of the Ninth Circuit ordered ICE to advise the court as to whether ICE planned to exercise prosecutorial discretion in five pending cases.[158] The court did so *sua sponte*, without such an order having been requested, and the dissenting judge expressed concern that the majority's order could portend future scrutiny of why ICE made particular decisions.[159] The dissent also asserted that judicial review of ICE's exercise of prosecutorial discretion is "sharply limited by the separation of powers."[160]

CONCLUSION

Regardless of whether it is characterized as "prosecutorial discretion" or "enforcement discretion," immigration officers are generally seen as having wide latitude in determining when, how, and even whether to pursue apparent violations of the INA. This latitude is similar to that possessed by prosecutors in the criminal law enforcement context and enforcement officials in other federal agencies. Whether and how to constrain this discretion has been a recurring issue for some Members of Congress, particularly in light of the June 2011 DHS memorandum on prosecutorial discretion and the more recent DACA initiative.[161] While some Members have expressed support for the DACA initiative,[162] or called for expanded use of prosecutorial discretion by immigration authorities in other contexts,[163] others have sought to prohibit DHS from granting deferred action or extended voluntary departure to removable aliens except in narrow circumstances,[164] or to "nullify" particular policies regarding prosecutorial discretion that have been articulated by the Obama Administration.[165]

The extent to which Congress can constrain the Administration's exercise of discretion in the DACA context, in particular, may depend on whether a reviewing court characterizes the underlying authority for the implementation of the program as constitutionally or statutorily based. Congress has broad authority to restrict discretionary acts taken pursuant to statutory delegations, while arguably limited authority, under the doctrine of Separation of Powers, to restrict the President's exercise of constitutionally based discretion. In addition, the degree of intrusion into executive enforcement decisions may also impact a court's review of any congressional response. For example, legal precedent suggests that Congress probably cannot directly limit the President's exercise of discretion by requiring that the executive branch initiate enforcement actions against particular individuals.[166] On the other hand, Congress would appear to have considerable latitude in establishing statutory guidelines for immigration officials to follow in the exercise of their enforcement powers, including by "indicat[ing] with precision the measures available to enforce the" INA, or by prohibiting DHS from considering certain factors in setting enforcement priorities.[167]

However, the existing judicial presumption that "an agency's decision not to take enforcement action [is] immune from judicial review,"[168] and the deference potentially accorded to an agency's interpretation of its governing statute,[169] suggests that such statutory guidelines would likely need to be clear, express, and specific. The use of "shall" in a provision of the INA may not, in itself, suffice for a statute to be construed as having provided enforceable guidelines for immigration officials to follow in exercising prosecutorial discretion. Absent a substantive legislative response, Congress may still be able to influence the implementation of DACA or other discretion-based policies by the immigration authorities, including by engaging in stringent oversight over the DHS program or by exercising its "power of the purse"[170] to prohibit DHS and its components from implementing particular policies related to the exercise of prosecutorial discretion that Congress does not support.[171]

End Notes

[1] U.S. Dep't of Justice, United States Attorneys' Manual, §9-27.110(B) (2002), available at http://www.justice.gov/ usao/eousa/foia_reading_room/usam/title9/27mcrm.htm#9-27.110.

[2] See, e.g., Julie L. Myers, Assistant Secretary, U.S. Immigration and Customs Enforcement (ICE), Prosecutorial and Custody Detention, Nov. 7, 2007, available at http://niwaplibrary. wcl.american.edu/reference/additional-materials/ immigration/enforcement-detention-and-criminal-justice/government-documents/Myers-Memo-Custody-Discretion-11- 7-07.pdf ("This memorandum serves to highlight the importance of exercising prosecutorial discretion when making administrative arrest and custody determinations for aliens who are nursing mothers."); Doris Meissner, Commissioner, INS, Exercising Prosecutorial Discretion, Nov. 7, 2000, available at http://niwaplibrary.wcl.american.edu/reference/ additional-materials/immigration/enforcement-detention-and-criminal-justice/government-documents/22092970-INSGuidance-Memo-Prosecutorial-Discretion-Doris-Meissner-11-7-00.pdf [hereinafter "2002 INS Guidance"] ("This memorandum describes the principles with which the INS exercises prosecutorial discretion and the process to be followed in making and monitoring discretionary decisions."). INS was abolished in 2002, and most of its functions were transferred to the newly created Department of Homeland by the Homeland Security Act of 2002 (P.L. 107-296).

[3] See, e.g., Crane v. Napolitano, No. 3:12-cv-03247-O, Amended Complaint (filed N.D. Tex., Oct. 10, 2012), at ¶¶ 88 89 ("U.S. Citizenship and Immigration Services is not a law enforcement agency. A non-law-enforcement agency cannot exercise prosecutorial discretion."): Robert J. Delahunty & John C. Yoo, The Obama Administration, the DREAM Act, and the Take Care Clause, at 3, available at http://papers.ssrn.com/sol3/ papers. cfm?abstract_id=2144031 (noting that immigration laws are primarily enforced civilly).

[4] See, e.g., Heckler v. Chaney, 470 U.S. 821, 831 (1985) ("[W]e recognize that an agency's refusal to institute proceedings shares to some extent the characteristics of the decision of a prosecutor in the Executive Branch not to indict—a decision which has long been regarded as the special province of the Executive Branch, inasmuch as it is the Executive who is charged by the Constitution to 'take Care that the Laws be faithfully executed.'").

[5] See, e.g., Lynda J. Oswald, Extended Voluntary Departure: Limiting the Attorney General's Discretion in Immigration Matters, 85 MICH. L. REV. 152, 158 n.40 (1986).

[6] U.S. Dep't of Homeland Security, Press Release, Notice Regarding I-9 Documentation Requirements for Hiring Hurricane Victims, Sept. 6, 2005, available at http://v2011.nilc. org/disaster_assistance/FINAL_I-9_Press_Release.pdf.

[7] The Obama Administration has also cited prosecutorial discretion in abstaining from prosecutions for contempt of Congress and violations of the Controlled Substances Act relating to the possession of marijuana. See Letter from James M. Cole, Deputy Attorney General, to John Boehner, Speaker of the House, June 28, 2012; Memorandum for Selected U.S. Attorneys from David W. Ogden, Deputy Attorney General, Investigations and Prosecutions in States Authorizing the Medical Use of Marijuana, Oct. 19, 2009; CRS Legal Sidebar, Obama Administration Will Not Challenge State Marijuana Laws That Do Not Undermine Federal Enforcement Priorities, by Brian T. Yeh and Todd Garvey, available at http://www.crs.gov/LegalSidebar/details.aspx?ID=664&Source=search.

[8] John Morton, Director, ICE, Civil Immigration Enforcement: Priorities for the Apprehension, Detention, and Removal of Aliens, Mar. 2, 2011, at 1-2, available at http://www.ice.gov/ doclib/news/releases/2011/ 110302washingtondc.pdf (aliens who have been convicted of crimes, are at least 16 years of age and participate in organized criminal gangs, are subject to outstanding criminal warrants, or "otherwise pose a serious risk to public safety" constituting the highest priorities for removal).

[9] John Morton, Director, ICE, Exercising Prosecutorial Discretion Consistent with the Civil Immigration Enforcement Priorities of the Agency for the Apprehension, Detention, and

Removal of Aliens, June 17, 2011, available at http://www.ice.gov/doclib/secure-communities/pdf/prosecutorial-discretion-memo.pdf [hereinafter "2011 DHS Guidance"].

[10] Janet Napolitano, Secretary of Homeland Security, Exercising Prosecutorial Discretion with Respect to Individuals Who Came to the United States as Children, June 15, 2012, at 1, available at http://www.dhs.gov/xlibrary/assets/s1- exercising-prosecutorial-discretion-individuals-who-came-to-us-as-children.pdf.

[11] U.S. ICE, Facilitating Parental Interests in the Course of Civil Immigration Enforcement Activities, No. 306-112- 002b, Aug. 23, 2013, available at http://www.ice.gov/doclib/detention-reform/pdf/ parental_interest_directive_signed.pdf.

[12] See, e.g., "Does Administrative Amnesty Harm Our Efforts to Gain and Maintain Operational Control of the Border?" Hearing Before the House Committee on Homeland Security, Subcommittee on Border and Maritime Security, Oct. 4, 2011; "U.S. Immigration and Customs Enforcement: Priorities and the Rule of Law," Hearing Before the House Committee on the Judiciary, Oct. 12, 2011.

[13] See, e.g., Testimony of Senator Michael S. Lee Before the House Committee on the Judiciary, "The Obama Administration's Abuse of Power," Sept. 12, 2012, at 5, available at http://judiciary.house.gov/hearings/ Hearings%202012/Lee%2009122012.pdf; The Obama Administration, the DREAM Act, and the Take Care Clause, supra note 3, at 5 (noting that the DREAM Act, "in one form or other, has been before Congress since 2001").

[14] See Crane, Amended Complaint, supra note 3. For further discussion of this litigation, see infra notes 119-120 and accompanying text. Two other suits challenging DACA were dismissed because the plaintiffs lacked standing. See Peterson v. President of the United States, No. 1:2012cv00257, Order Granting Motion to Dismiss (D.N.H., Oct. 22, 2012); Dutkiewicz v. Napolitano, No. 8:2012cv01447, Order Granting Motion to Dismiss (M.D. Fla., Nov. 9, 2012).

[15] See, e.g., Restrepo v. Holder, 676 F.3d 10 (1st Cir. 2012) (cancellation of removal pursuant to 8 U.S.C. §1229b(a) is solely within the Attorney General's discretion absent a colorable constitutional claim or a question of law); Bo Cooper, General Counsel, INS, INS Exercise of Prosecutorial Discretion, July 11, 2000, at 4, available at http://niwaplibrary. wcl.american.edu/reference/additional-materials/immigration/enforcement-detention-and-criminaljustice/government-documents/Bo-Cooper-memo%20pros%2 0discretion7.11. 2000.pdf ("The doctrine of prosecutorial discretion applies to enforcement decisions, not benefit decisions. For example, a decision to charge, or not to charge, an alien with a ground of deportability is clearly a prosecutorial enforcement decision. By contrast, the grant of an immigration benefit, such as naturalization or adjustment of status, is a benefit decision that is not a subject for prosecutorial discretion.").

[16] See, e.g., Nat'l Fed'n of Indep. Bus. v. Sebelius,—U.S.—, 132 S. Ct. 2566, 2600 (2012) (describing regulation of immigration as among Congress's powers under the Commerce Clause); Arizona v. United States,—U.S.—132 S. Ct. 2492, 2498 (2012) (authority to regulate immigration resting, in part, on the power to establish a uniform rule of naturalization); Henderson v. Mayor of New York, 92 U.S. 259 (1876) (striking down New York and Louisiana laws that required shipmasters to pay fees or post bonds to indemnify states if immigrants ended up on public assistance on the grounds that the laws interfered with Congress's power to regulate interstate commerce); Chy Lung v. Freeman, 92 U.S. 275 (1875) (striking down a California law regulating the entry of "lewd and debauched women" on the grounds that it interfered with Congress's power to regulate the admission of noncitizens); The Passenger Cases, 48 U.S. 283 (1849) (striking down New York and

Massachusetts laws that levied fees on arriving immigrant passengers, in part, on the grounds that such fees constituted unconstitutional regulations of foreign commerce).

[17] See, e.g., The Chinese Exclusion Case, 130 U.S. 581, 604 (1889) (listing the powers to "declare war, make treaties, suppress insurrection, repel invasion, regulate foreign commerce, secure republican governments to the States, and admit subjects of other nations to citizenship" as authorizing Congress to enact legislation excluding Chinese laborers); Fong Yue Ting v. United States, 149 U.S. 698, 705-09 (1893) (relying on the same sources to affirm Congress's power to deport noncitizens). See also Arizona, 132 S. Ct. at 2514 (Scalia, J., dissenting) (citing the Migration or Importation Clause as a source of federal power over immigration). This clause, which pertains directly to slavery, can be seen as addressing federal power to control the entry of certain persons into the United States.

[18] Arizona, 132 S. Ct. at 2498; Nishimara Ekiu v. United States, 142 U.S. 651, 659 (1892) ("It is an accepted maxim of international law, that every sovereign nation has the power, as inherent in sovereignty, and essential to self-preservation, to forbid the entrance of foreigners within its dominions, or to admit them only in such cases and upon such conditions as it may see fit to prescribe.").

[19] In particular, the Constitution grants the treaty power to the President. See U.S. Const., art. II, §2 ("[The President] shall have [the] Power, by and with the Advice and Consent of the Senate to make Treaties ...").

[20] See, e.g., Sale v. Haitian Centers Council, Inc., 509 U.S. 155, 201 (1993) ("Congress ... has plenary power over immigration matters."); INS v. Chadha, 462 U.S. 919, 940-41 (1983) ("The plenary authority of Congress over aliens under Art. I, §8, cl. 4, is not open to question."); Boutilier v. INS, 387 U.S. 118, 123 (1967) ("The Court without exception has sustained Congress' 'plenary power to make rules for the admission of aliens.'").

[21] Oceanic Navigation Co. v. Stranahan, 214 U.S. 320, 339 (1909). This passage has been quoted in numerous other cases. See, e.g., Reno v. Flores, 507 U.S. 292, 305 (1993); Fiallo v. Bell, 430 U.S. 787, 792 (1977); Kleindienst v. Mandel, 408 U.S. 753, 766 (1972); Hana v. Gonzales, 503 F.3d 39, 43 (1st Cir. 2007).

[22] Some commentators have suggested that the language in these cases may have been partially motivated by a desire to enforce a more robust conception of the nondelegation doctrine. See, e.g., Adam B. Cox and Cristina M. Rodriguez, The President and Immigration Law, 119 YALE L.J. 458, 474 n.46 (2009).

[23] 509 U.S. 155 (1993).

[24] Id. at 201.

[25] Lem Moon Sing v. United States, 158 U.S. 538, 547 (1895) (finding that the Act of 1894, which declared that the decisions of the appropriate immigration or custom officers regarding the right of aliens to enter this country are generally final, took away the court's authority to review such decisions). See also Galvan v. Press, 347 U.S. 522, 531 (1954) ("In the enforcement of these policies, the Executive Branch of the Government must respect the procedural safeguards of due process. But that the formulation of these policies is entrusted exclusively to Congress has become about as firmly embedded in the legislative and judicial tissue of our body politic as any aspect of our government.").

[26] Mahler v. Eby, 264 U.S. 32, 43-45 (1924) (finding that certain deportation orders issued by the Secretary of Labor were void because the orders did not indicate that the Secretary had made certain findings required by statute). See also Kleindienst, 408 U.S. at 769 ("[W]e think the Attorney General validly exercised the plenary power that Congress delegated to the Executive by [certain provisions of the INA]."); Ng Fung Ho v. White, 259 U.S. 276, 280 (1922) ("Congress has power to order at any time the deportation of aliens whose

presence in the country it deems hurtful; and may do so by appropriate executive proceedings."); The Japanese Immigrant Case, 189 U.S. 86, 98 (1903) ("As to [aliens outside the United States], the decisions of executive or administrative officers, acting within powers expressly conferred by Congress, are due process of law."); Nishimura Ekiu, 142 U.S. at 659 ("The supervision of the admission of aliens into the United States may be entrusted by Congress either to the Department of State, having the general management of foreign relations, or to the Department of the Treasury, charged with the enforcement of the laws regulating foreign commerce; and Congress has often passed acts forbidding the immigration of particular classes of foreigners, and has committed the execution of these acts to the Secretary of the Treasury, to collectors of customs and to inspectors acting under their authority.").

[27] Cf. The President and Immigration Law, supra note 22, at 510 ("[M]odern courts and commentators have largely ignored the question of power allocation between the President and Congress."); The Obama Administration, the DREAM Act, and the Take Care Clause, supra note 3, at 3 (noting that the Constitution does not explicitly allocate authority over immigration among the political branches). Only in the case of INS v. Chadha did the Supreme Court confront a separation of powers question touching upon immigration. 462 U.S. 919 (1983). At issue in Chadha was the permissibility of a statutory provision which authorized either house of Congress, by resolution, to invalidate the executive branch's determination to suspend deportation and adjust the status of aliens whose deportation would result in "extreme hardship" to the alien or the alien's family. The Court struck the statute down on separation of powers grounds, finding that it violated the constitutional requirement that legislative acts be passed by both houses of Congress and presented for the President's approval. In reaching this conclusion, the Court noted both Congress's "plenary authority" over aliens, and that the "Attorney General acts in his presumptively Article II capacity when he administers the [INA]." Id. at 940, 953 n.16. It is unclear, however, whether the reference to the Attorney General's "Article II capacity" means prosecutorial discretion under the Take Care Clause, or some other authority of the executive.

[28] See, e.g., United States v. Valenzuela-Bernal, 458 U.S. 858, 864 (1982) ("The power to regulate immigration—an attribute of sovereignty essential to the preservation of any nation—has been entrusted by the Constitution to the political branches of the Federal Government."); Mathews v. Diaz, 426 U.S. 67, 81 (1976) ("[T]he relationship between the U.S. and our alien visitors has been committed to the political branches of the federal government. Since decisions in these matters may implicate our relations with foreign powers ... such decisions are frequently of a character more appropriate to either the Legislature or the Executive branches than to the Judiciary."); The Chinese Exclusion Case, 130 U.S. 581, 607-09 (1889) (rejecting the alien's assertion that the federal government lacked the power to regulate immigration, in part, because the "political department" of the United States had the responsibility for determining "who shall compose [society's] members").

[29] 338 U.S. 537, 542 (1950).

[30] 426 U.S. 88, 103 (1976). Following the Court's decision, President Ford issued an executive order reestablishing these employment restrictions. Exec. Order No. 11, 935, 41 Fed. Reg. 37301 (Sept. 2, 1976). When challenged, this order was found to be within the President's authority. Vergara v. Hampton, 581 F.2d 1281 (7th Cir. 1978). However, in so finding, the reviewing court emphasized the President's statutory authority under 5 U.S.C. §3301(1), not any inherent authority over immigration or aliens.

[31] Hampton, 426 U.S. at 104 ("In this case the petitioners have identified several interests which the Congress or the President might deem sufficient to justify the exclusion of noncitizens from the federal service. They argue, for example, that the broad exclusion may facilitate the President's negotiation of treaties with foreign powers by enabling him to offer employment opportunities to citizens of a given foreign country in exchange for reciprocal concessions.").

[32] Any assertion of inherent, independent, or implied constitutional presidential authority in the field of immigration may be evaluated under the rubric established by Justice Jackson's concurring opinion in Youngstown Sheet & Tube Co. v. Sawyer, 343 U.S. 579 (1952). The Youngstown framework, which the Court has characterized as bringing "together as much combination of analysis and common sense as there is in this area," has generally been applied when a President seeks to take action within an area generally considered to be within Congress's purview. See, e.g., Dames & Moore v. Regan, 453 U.S. 654, 661-62 (1981). Importantly, the scope of executive authority under the Jackson analysis is judged in direct relation to congressional action in the field. When the President acts pursuant to an authorization from Congress, his power is "at its maximum." To the contrary, when the President seeks to take action that conflicts with Congress's expressed will, his power is at its "lowest ebb, for then he can rely only upon his own constitutional powers minus any constitutional powers of Congress over the matter." Where Congress is silent, "there is a zone of twilight in which he and Congress may have concurrent authority, or in which its distribution is uncertain." Youngstown, 343 U.S. at 635-37. Any claimed constitutional authority justifying executive action in the field of immigration would, therefore, likely be evaluated in relation to the policies established by Congress in the INA and other pertinent statutes.

[33] See, e.g., United States v. Armstrong, 517 U.S. 456, 464 (1996) (noting that the Attorney General and the United States Attorneys have wide latitude in enforcing federal criminal law because "they are designated by statute as the President's delegates to help him discharge his constitutional duty to 'take Care that the Laws be faithfully executed'"); Heckler, 470 U.S. at 831 ("[W]e recognize that an agency's refusal to institute proceedings shares to some extent the characteristics of the decision of a prosecutor in the Executive Branch not to indict—a decision which has long been regarded as the special province of the Executive Branch, inasmuch as it is the Executive who is charged by the Constitution to 'take Care that the Laws be faithfully executed.'").

[34] An argument could also potentially be made that Congress has impliedly delegated the authority to exercise certain types of discretion to the executive branch since it has been aware of the practice, and could be said to have acquiesced. See, e.g., Johns v. Dep't of Justice, 653 F.2d 884, 890 (5th Cir. 1981) ("Deportation is not, however, the inevitable consequence of unauthorized presence in the United States. The Attorney General is given discretion by express statutory provisions, in some situations, to ameliorate the rigidity of the deportation laws. In other instances, as the result of implied authority, he exercises discretion nowhere granted expressly.").

[35] Texas v. United States, 106 F.3d 661, 667 (5th Cir. 1997) (rejecting allegations that the Attorney General had breached his nondiscretionary duty under the INA to control immigration, in part, on the grounds that enforcement of the INA is committed to the Attorney General's discretion). See also Hotel & Rest. Employees Union Local 25 v. Smith, 846 F.2d 1499, 1510 (D.C. Cir. 1988) (citing Section 103(a)(3) to support the proposition that the then-Attorney General enjoyed "broad latitude in enforcing the immigration laws,"

and that the decision to grant or withhold extended voluntary departure "falls within this broad mandate"), aff'g, 563 F. Supp. 157 (D.D.C. 1983).

[36] Crane v. Napolitano, No. 3:12-CV-3247-O, Defendants' Motion to Dismiss and Memorandum in Support (filed N.D. Tex., Nov. 13, 2012). The INS had previously expressed the view that Section 242(g) of the INA meant that it had discretion not to pursue removal against an alien because such decisions are not judicially reviewable. See INS Exercise of Prosecutorial Discretion, supra note 15, at 9. However, DHS does not appear to rely upon this argument at present.

[37] INA §212(a)(9)(B); 8 U.S.C. §1182(a)(9)(B). Any such waivers may only be granted where certain conditions are met (e.g., the refusal of admission to the alien would result in "extreme hardship" to his or her citizen or LPR relatives).

[38] INA §274a(h)(3); 8 U.S.C. §1324a(h)(3).

[39] See, e.g., Wayte v. United States, 470 U.S. 598, 607 (1985) ("In our criminal justice system, the Government retains 'broad discretion' as to whom to prosecute.") (citing United States v. Goodwin, 457 U.S. 368, 380 (1982)); United States v. Nixon, 418 U.S. 683, 693 (1974) ("[T]he Executive Branch has exclusive authority and absolute discretion to decide whether to prosecute a case...") (citing the Confiscation Cases, 74 U.S. 454 (1869)).

[40] See, e.g., Rebecca Krauss, The Theory of Prosecutorial Discretion in Federal Law: Origins and Development, 6 SETON HALL CIR. REV. 1, 19-26 (2009) (describing the English use of the nolle prosequi and its "absorb[tion]" by American law).

[41] Id. at 20.

[42] See, e.g., Confiscation Cases, 74 U.S. 454 (1869); Newman v. United States, 382 F.2d 479, 480 (D.C. Cir. 1967) ("Most recently, the issue of the United States Attorney's 'discretionary control of criminal prosecutions has arisen in connection with the filing of a nolle prosequi, and the Courts have regularly refused to interfere with these voluntary dismissals of prosecution.'") (citing Louis B. Schwartz, Federal Criminal Jurisdiction and Prosecutors' Discretion, 13 LAW & CONTEMP. PROB. 64, 83 (1948)). Today, judicial approval is generally required before a prosecutor may dismiss an ongoing prosecution. See FED. R. CRIM. P. 48(a) ("The government may, with leave of court, dismiss an indictment, information, or complaint.").

[43] U.S. Const. Art. II, §3 ("[H]e shall take Care that the Laws be faithfully executed.... ").

[44] See, e.g., Armstrong, 517 U.S. at 464 ("They have this latitude because they are designated by statute as the President's delegates to help him discharge his constitutional responsibility to 'take Care that the Laws be faithfully executed.'"); Confiscation Cases, 74 U.S. at 458 ("Appointed, as the Attorney General is, in pursuance of an act of Congress, to prosecute and conduct such suits, argument would seem to be unnecessary to prove his authority to dispose of these cases in the manner proposed.... "); Ponzi v. Fessenden, 258 U.S. 254, 262 (1922) ("The Attorney General is the head of the Department of Justice. He is the hand of the President in taking care that the laws of the United States in protection of the interests of the United States in legal proceedings and in the prosecution of offences be faithfully executed."); United States v. Cox, 342 F.2d 167, 171 (5th Cir. 1965) ("The Attorney General is the hand of the President in taking care that the laws of the United States in legal proceedings and in the prosecution of offenses, be faithfully executed. Although as a member of the bar, the attorney for the United States is an officer of the court, he is nevertheless an executive official of the Government, and it is as an officer of the executive department that he exercises discretion as to whether or not there shall be a prosecution in a particular case. It follows, as an incident of the constitutional separation of powers, that the courts are not to interfere with the free exercise of the discretionary powers of the attorneys

of the United States in their control over criminal prosecutions.") (internal citations omitted)).

[45] Wayte, 470 U.S. at 607. However, the U.S. Court of Appeals for the District of Columbia Circuit has observed that "the decisions of this court have never allowed the phrase 'prosecutorial discretion' to be treated as a magical incantation which automatically provides a shield for arbitrariness." Med. Comm. for Human Rights v. SEC, 432 F.2d 659, 673 (D.C. Cir. 1970).

[46] See Prosecution for Contempt of Congress of an Executive Branch Official Who Has Asserted a Claim of Executive Privilege, 8 OP. OFF. LEGAL COUNSEL 101, 114 (1984) (emphasis added). This traditional conception may, however, have been qualified in some respects following the Supreme Court's decision in Morrison v. Olson, in which the Court upheld a congressional delegation of prosecutorial power to an "independent counsel" under the Ethics in Government Act. In sustaining the validity of the statute's appointment and removal conditions, the Court suggested that although the independent counsel's prosecutorial powers—including the "no small amount of discretion and judgment [exercised by the counsel] in deciding how to carry out his or her duties under the Act"—were executive in that they had "typically" been performed by executive branch officials, the court did not consider such an exercise of prosecutorial power to be "so central to the functioning of the Executive Branch" as to require Presidential control over the independent counsel. 487 U.S. 654 (1988). While the ultimate reach of Morrison may be narrow in that the independent counsel was granted only limited jurisdiction and was still subject to the supervision of the Attorney General, it does appear that Congress may vest certain prosecutorial powers, including the exercise of prosecutorial discretion, in an executive branch official who is independent of traditional presidential controls. But see Nixon, 418 U.S. at 693 ("[T]he Executive Branch has exclusive authority and absolute discretion to decide whether to prosecute a case.... ").

[47] Heckler, 470 U.S. at 832. The Court also expressed concern that judicial review of agencies' exercise of prosecutorial discretion could impose "systemic costs" by delaying criminal proceedings, chilling law enforcement, and undermining prosecutorial effectiveness. Id. at 833.

[48] Id. at 831. Accordingly, such decisions are generally precluded from judicial review under the Administrative Procedure Act (APA). 5 U.S.C. §701 (establishing an exception to the APA's presumption of reviewability where "agency action is committed to agency discretion by law").

[49] Heckler, 470 U.S. at 831.

[50] Id. at 832.

[51] Id. at 833.

[52] 525 U.S. 471, 490 (1999). See also Shaughnessy, 338 U.S. at 543 (noting that immigration is a "field where flexibility and the adaptation of the congressional policy to infinitely variable conditions constitute the essence of the program").

[53] See, e.g., Padilla v. Kentucky,—U.S.—, 130 S. Ct. 1473, 1481 (2010) ("We have long recognized that deportation is a particularly severe 'penalty,' but it is not, in a strict sense, a criminal sanction.") (internal citations omitted); INS v. Lopez-Mendoza, 468 U.S. 1032, 1038-39 (1984) ("A deportation proceeding is a purely civil action to determine eligibility to remain in this country, not to punish an unlawful entry.... The purpose of deportation is not to punish past transgressions but rather to put an end to a continuing violation of the immigration laws.").

[54] Specifically, the Court noted that any delays in criminal proceedings caused by judicial review of exercises of prosecutorial discretion would "merely ... postpone the criminal's receipt of his just desserts," while delays in removal proceedings would "permit and prolong a continuing violation of United States law," and could potentially permit the alien to acquire a basis for changing his or her status. Reno, 525 U.S. at 490. The Court further noted that immigration proceedings are unique in that they can implicate foreign policy objectives and foreign-intelligence techniques that are generally not implicated in criminal proceedings. Id. at 491. It also found that the interest in avoiding selective or otherwise improper prosecution in immigration proceedings, discussed below, is "less compelling" than in criminal proceedings because deportation is not a punishment and may be "necessary to bring to an end an ongoing violation of United States law." Id. (emphasis in original).

[55] Arizona, 132 S. Ct. at 2498. Justice Scalia's dissenting opinion, in contrast, specifically cited Secretary Napolitano's memorandum regarding the exercise of prosecutorial discretion with respect to certain aliens who came to the United States as children when asserting that "there is no reason why the Federal Executive's need to allocate its scarce enforcement resources should disable Arizona from devoting its resources to illegal immigration in Arizona that in its view the Federal Executive has given short shrift." Id. at 2520 (Scalia, J., dissenting) (emphasis in original)).

[56] Arizona, 132 S. Ct. at 2499.

[57] Assa'ad v. U.S. Attorney General, 332 F.3d 1321, 1339 (11th Cir. 2003); Matter of Artigas, 23 I. & N. Dec. 99 (BIA 2001) (Filppu, J., dissenting). DHS grants an alien parole when it permits the alien to physically enter the United States and to remain as a matter of sufferance only, and without having made an "entry," for "urgent humanitarian reasons or significant public benefit." INA §212(d)(5)(A); 8 U.S.C. §1182(d)(5)(A).

[58] Hanggi v. Holder, 563 F.3d 378, 383 (8th Cir. 2009); Rodrigues v. Attorney General of the United States, 414 Fed. App'x 484, 488 (3d Cir. 2011); Matter of Avetisyan, 25 I. & N. Dec. 688 (BIA 2012); Matter of Bahta, 22 I. & N. Dec. 1381 (BIA 2000); Matter of Singh, 21 I. & N. Dec. 427 (BIA 1996); Matter of Ruis, 18 I. & N. Dec. 320 (BIA 1982); Matter of Roussis, 18 I. & N. Dec. 256 (BIA 1982); Matter of Lennon, 15 I. & N. Dec. 9 (BIA 1974).

[59] Matter of Lujan-Quintana, 25 I. & N. Dec. 53 (BIA 2009). But see Flores-Ledezma v. Gonzales, 415 F.3d 375, 382 (5th Cir. 2005) ("Although we decline at this juncture to equate the Attorney General's discretion to choose which proceeding a non-LPR will receive with prosecutorial discretion, it is fully convincing that the Government has highlighted a rational basis for the Attorney General's exercise of such discretion."). Section 240 of the INA provides for formal removal proceedings. However, "expedited removal," without formal proceedings, is also possible in the case of certain aliens seeking admission to the United States. INA §235(b); 8 U.S.C. §1225(b).

[60] Matter of G-N-C, 22 I. & N. Dec. 281 (BIA 1998). See also Akhtar v. Gonzales, 450 F.3d 587, 591 (5th Cir. 2006) (whether to terminate removal proceedings to allow the alien to apply for immigration benefits that may potentially be available).

[61] Hotel & Rest. Employees Union Local 25, 846 F.2d at 1510-11; Barahona-Gomez v. Reno, 236 F.3d 1115, 1119 n.3 (9th Cir. 2001); Johnson v. INS, 962 F.2d 574, 579 (7th Cir. 1992); Carmona Martinez v. Ashcroft, 118 Fed. App'x 238, 239 (9th Cir. 2004); Matter of Yauri, 25 I. & N. Dec. 103 (BIA 2009); Matter of Singh, 21 I. & N. Dec. 427 (BIA 1996); Matter of Luviano-Rodriguez, 21 I. & N. Dec. 235 (BIA 1996); Matter of Quintero, 18 I. & N. Dec. 348 (BIA 1982).

[62] Matter of Avetisyan, 25 I. & N. Dec. 688 (BIA 2012); Matter of York, 22 I. & N. Dec. 660 (BIA 1999); Matter of Joseph, 22 I. & N. Dec. 660 (BIA 1990).

[63] Matter of Joseph, 22 I. & N. Dec. 660 (BIA 1999).

[64] Matter of M/V Saru Meru, 20 I. & N. Dec. 592 (BIA 1992); Matter of M/V Solemn Judge, 18 I. & N. Dec. 186 (BIA 1982).

[65] Shoba Sivaprasad Wadhia, The Role of Prosecutorial Discretion in Immigration Law, 9 CONN. PUB. INT. L.J. 243, 263 (2010) (quoting a 2009 DHS press release on relief for widows of U.S. citizens). Individual aliens may request that they be granted deferred action (formerly known as non-priority status), or immigration officials may decide, sua sponte, to defer action.

[66] See, e.g., Exercising Prosecutorial Discretion with Respect to Individuals Who Came to the United States as Children, supra note 10; John Morton, Director, ICE, Prosecutorial Discretion: Certain Victims, Witnesses, and Plaintiffs, June 17, 2011, available at http://www.ice.gov/doclib/secure-communities/pdf/domestic-violence.pdf; Prosecutorial and Custody Detention, supra note 2.

[67] See, e.g., Extended Voluntary Departure, supra note 5, at 155-59.

[68] See, e.g., 2011 DHS Guidance, supra note 9, at 2-3; Civil Immigration Enforcement, supra note 8, at 3; Prosecutorial Discretion: Certain Victims, Witnesses, and Plaintiffs, supra note 66, at 2; William J. Howard, Principal Legal Advisor, ICE, Prosecutorial Discretion, Oct. 24, 2005, at 2, available at http://niwaplibrary.wcl.american.edu/reference/ additional-materials/immigration/enforcement-detention-and-criminal-justice/government-documents/22092975-ICEGuidance-Memo-Prosecutorial-Discretion-William-J-Howard-10-24-05.pdf; 2002 INS Guidance, supra note 2.

[69] See, e.g., Applicability of Prosecutorial Discretion Memoranda to Certain Family Relationships, supra note 11 ("This and other memoranda related to prosecutorial discretion are designed to ensure that agency resources are focused on our enforcement priorities, including individuals who pose a threat to public safety, are recent border crossers, or repeatedly violate our immigration laws."); Civil Immigration Enforcement, supra note 8, at 1 ("ICE ... only has resources to remove approximately 400,000 aliens per year, less than 4 percent of the estimated illegal alien population of the United States."); Prosecutorial Discretion, supra note 68 (noting demands created by the establishment of DHS and the increasing number of immigration cases being litigated in federal courts).

[70] See, e.g., 2011 DHS Guidance, supra note 9, at 4 (noting that factors to consider include the alien's length of presence in the United States; the circumstances of the alien's arrival in the United States; the alien's pursuit of education in the United States; the alien's ties and contributions to the community; whether the alien or the alien's spouse is pregnant or nursing, or suffers from a severe mental or physical illness; and conditions in the alien's home country); Prosecutorial Discretion, supra note 68 (aliens who are immediate relatives of members of the U.S. military; aliens who have citizen children with serious medical conditions or disabilities; aliens who are undergoing treatment for a potentially life-threatening illness).

[71] See, e.g., 2011 DHS Guidance, supra note 9, at 2.

[72] See, e.g., 2002 INS Guidance, supra note 2, at 4.

[73] See, e.g., id. at 6.

[74] See, e.g., 2011 DHS Guidance, supra note 9, at 3. One particular area where such policies have shifted over time is whether immigration attorneys have the authority to cancel Notices to Appear issued by immigration officers.

[75] 2011 DHS Guidance, supra note 9, at 4. See also Civil Immigration Enforcement, supra note 8, at 4.

[76] 2011 DHS Guidance, supra note 9, at 5; Prosecutorial and Custody Detention, supra note 2; 2002 INS Guidance, supra note 2, at 11.

[77] United States v. Batchelder, 442 U.S. 114, 125 (1979).

[78] See, e.g., Nader v. Saxbe, 497 F.2d 676, 679 (D.C. Cir. 1974) ("It would seem to follow that the exercise of prosecutorial discretion, like the exercise of Executive discretion generally, is subject to statutory and constitutional limits enforceable through judicial review.").

[79] DaimlerChrysler Corp. v. Cuno, 547 U.S. 332, 342 (2006) (quoting Allen v. Wright, 468 U.S. 737, 751 (1984)). The requirements as to injury, causation, and redressibility refer to Article III standing. Some courts have also found that plaintiffs challenging certain actions in the immigration context lack prudential standing to enforce the INA. See, e.g., Fed'n for Am. Immigration Reform v. Reno, 93 F.3d 897, 900 (D.C. Cir. 1996) (plaintiffs were not within the zone of interests protected by the INA for purposes of their claim that a "rush of immigrants adversely affects the welfare of the Federation's members by generating unemployment and wage reductions"). Recently, one federal district court did find that the ICE agents challenging the DACA initiative satisfy the prudential standing requirements because the statutory provisions which they claim are violated by DACA also govern their conduct in managing investigations and initiating removal proceedings. See Crane v. Napolitano, 920 F. Supp. 2d 724, 740-41 (N.D. Tex. 2013). However, this court subsequently found that the ICE agents' claims are within the exclusive jurisdiction of the Merit Systems Protection Board (MSPB), because their alleged injury was "being compelled to violate a federal statute upon pain of adverse employment action." Crane, No. 3:12-cv-03247-O, Order (N.D. Tex., July 31, 2013), available at http://www.crs.gov/analysis/legalsidebar/Documents/Crane_DenialofMotionforReconsideration.pdf.

[80] See, e.g., Lance v. Coffman, 549 U.S. 437, 439 (2007) ("A plaintiff raising only a generally available grievance about government—claiming only harm to his and every citizen's interest in [the] proper application of the Constitution and laws, and seeking relief that no more directly [or] tangibly benefits him than it does the public at large—does not state an Article III case or controversy.") (internal quotations omitted)); Lujan v. Defenders of Wildlife, 504 U.S. 555, 562 (1992) ("[W]hen the plaintiff is not himself the object of the government action or inaction he challenges, standing is not precluded, but is ordinarily 'substantially more difficult' to establish."). Individual Members of Congress also generally lack standing to challenge presidential actions. In Raines v. Byrd, the Supreme Court held that in order to obtain standing an individual Member must assert either a personal injury, like the loss of his congressional seat, or an institutional injury that amounts to vote nullification, which requires that no other legislative remedy exists to redress the alleged injury. See 521 U.S. 811 (1997).

[81] See, e.g., Donelon v. La. Div. of Admin. Law ex rel. Wise, 522 F.3d 564 (5th Cir. 2008) (Louisiana Commissioner of Insurance lacked standing to challenge the constitutionality of a state law which he alleged violated the Constitution); Finch v. Miss. State Med. Ass'n, Inc., 585 F.2d 765, 773-75 (5th Cir. 1978) (governor of Mississippi lacked standing to challenge a state law whose enforcement, he believed, would cause him to violate his oath to uphold the federal and state constitutions).

[82] Compare Drake v. Obama, 664 F.3d 774, 780 (9th Cir. 2011) ("The notion that [the plaintiff] will be disciplined by the military for obeying President Obama's orders is entirely speculative. He might be disciplined for disobeying those orders, but he has an 'available course of action which subjects [him] to no concrete adverse consequences'—he can obey the orders of the Commander-in-Chief.") (emphasis in original)) and Crane, 920 F. Supp. 2d at 738 (finding that the ICE agents challenging DACA have "suffered an injury-in-fact by

virtue of being compelled to violate a federal statute upon pain of adverse employment action," and otherwise satisfy the requirements for standing). After finding that the plaintiffs have standing, and are likely to prevail on the merits of their claim that DACA violates the INA, the court in Crane ultimately found that it lacks jurisdiction because the ICE agents' claims are within the exclusive jurisdiction of the MSPB. Crane, Order, supra note 79.

[83] Donelon, 552 F.3d at 568 (emphasis in original).

[84] See, e.g., Miller v. Albright, 523 U.S. 420, 434 n.11 (1998) (plurality opinion); Fiallo, 430 U.S. at 796; Mathews, 426 U.S. at 82.

[85] See, e.g., Arizona, 132 S. Ct. at 2499.

[86] Negusie v. Holder, 555 U.S. 511, 517 (2009) ("The Attorney General's decision to bar an alien who has participated in persecution 'may affect our relations with [the alien's native] country or its neighbors. The judiciary is not well positioned to shoulder primary responsibility for assessing the likelihood and importance of such diplomatic repercussions."); INS v. Abudu, 485 U.S. 94, 110 (1988) ("Although all adjudications by administrative agencies are to some degree judicial and to some degree political ... INS officials must exercise especially sensitive political functions that implicate foreign relations.").

[87] Texas, 106 F.3d at 665 (dismissing a state's suit alleging that the federal government had violated the constitution and the INA by failing to control illegal immigration, in part, on the grounds that it was a political question). The political question doctrine is based on the notion that courts should refrain from deciding questions that the Constitution has entrusted to other branches of government. See, e.g., Marbury v. Madison, 5 U.S. (1 Cr.) 137, 170 (1803). In determining whether a case entails a political question, courts consider whether there is "[1] a textually demonstrable constitutional commitment of the issue to a coordinate political department; or [2] a lack of judicially discoverable and manageable standards for resolving it," among other things. Baker v. Carr, 369 U.S. 186, 217 (1962).

[88] Adams, 480 F.2d at 1162. See also Heckler, 470 U.S. at 832-33 n.4 (finding that judicial review of exercises of enforcement discretion could potentially be obtained in cases where an agency has adopted a general policy that is an "abdication of its statutory responsibilities").

[89] Bordenkircher v. Hayes, 434 U.S. 357, 364 (1977) (finding that a state prosecutor's decision to indict the defendant as habitual offender after he refused to plead guilty of a felony did not violate the defendant's constitutional rights).

[90] Goodwin, 457 U.S. at 372.

[91] 118 U.S. 356 (1886).

[92] Reno, 525 U.S. at 489 (quoting Armstrong, 517 U.S. at 463).

[93] Armstrong, 517 U.S. at 465.

[94] Reno, 525 U.S. at 490. It should be noted, however, that the Reno Court did not hold that discriminatory enforcement of the immigration laws does not offend the Equal Protection Clause, only that Section 242(g) of the INA (8 U.S.C. §1252(g)) deprives the courts of jurisdiction over such claims.

[95] Reno, 525 U.S. at 488.

[96] Id. at 473.

[97] Id. at 489 ("Even in the criminal-law field, a selective prosecution claim is a rara avis [rare bird].").

[98] Reno, 525 U.S. at 491.

[99] See, e.g., Matter of E-R-M & L-R-M, 25 I. & N. Dec. at 522.

[100] Adams, 480 F.2d at 1162.

[101] U.S. Const. art. II, §3. See also Kendall v. United States ex rel. Stokes, 37 U.S. 524, 613 ("To contend that the obligation imposed on the President to see the laws faithfully executed, implies a power to forbid their execution, is a novel construction of the constitution, and entirely inadmissible.").

[102] Texas, 106 F.3d at 667.

[103] Id.

[104] See, e.g., Crane, Amended Complaint, supra note 3, at ¶ 101 ("The application of 'deferred action' to approximately 15% of aliens who are in the United States without authorization is not an exercise of executive branch discretion permitted by the Constitution."); The Obama Administration, the DREAM Act, and the Take Care Clause, supra note 3, at 2 ("[I]f a President can refuse to enforce a federal law against a class of 800,000 to 1.76 million, what discernible limits are there to prosecutorial discretion?").

[105] Jeanne Batalova and Michelle Mittelstadt, Migration Policy Institute, Relief from Deportation: Demographic Profile of DREAMers Potentially Eligible under the Deferred Action Policy, Aug. 2012, available at http://www.migrationpolicy.org /pubs/ FS24_ deferredaction.pdf, at 1.

[106] Myers v. United States, 272 U.S. 52, 291-92 (1926) (Brandeis, J., dissenting). See also Heckler, 470 U.S. at 831 (noting that, among the factors that make agency decisions to refuse enforcement generally unsuitable for judicial review, are questions as to "whether agency resources are best spent on this violation or another, ... whether the particular enforcement action requested best fits the agency's overall policies, and ... whether the agency has enough resources to undertake the action at all").

[107] See, e.g., Michael Hoefer, Nancy Rytina, and Bryan Baker, DHS Office of Immigration Statistics, Estimates of the Unauthorized Immigrant Population Residing in the United States: January 2011, Population Estimates (Mar. 2012), available at http://www.dhs.gov/xlibrary/assets/statistics/publications/ois_ill_pe_2011.pdf.

[108] Civil Immigration Enforcement, supra note 8, at 1 ("ICE ... only has resources to remove approximately 400,000 aliens per year, less than 4 percent of the estimated illegal alien population in the United States."); Defendants' Motion to Dismiss and Memorandum in Support, supra note 36, at 19 ("Deferring action for certain childhood arrivals means nothing more than that the Department will shift its limited resources to focus on its highest removal priorities, which include, per Congress's directive, a focus on criminal aliens and other aliens who threaten public safety.").

[109] The Executive could also potentially still take enforcement action in the latter cases by, for example, commencing removal proceedings against aliens whom it had previously decided not to bring proceedings against. There is no statute of limitations for the removal of unlawfully present aliens, so those who currently are removable on the grounds that they are present without authorization would generally still be removable on these grounds in the future. However, by remaining in the country for a longer period of time, aliens who are present without authorization could potentially acquire new bases for adjusting status (e.g., marrying a U.S. citizen or lawful permanent resident), as the Court noted in Reno. 525 U.S. at 490. In addition, at least at some times previously, the immigration agencies had policies of not taking action against persons whom they had previously determined warranted favorable exercises of prosecutorial discretion unless the alien's circumstances had changed. See 2002 INS Guidance, supra note 2, at 11-12 (noting that favorable exercises of discretion are to be "clearly documented" in the alien's file, and that an INS office should generally abide by a favorable decision taken by another office on a matter, absent new or changed circumstances).

[110] Exercising Prosecutorial Discretion with Respect to Individuals Who Came to the United States as Children, supra note 10, at 2 ("No individual should receive deferred action under this memorandum unless they first pass a background check and requests for relief pursuant to this memorandum are to be decided on a case by case basis. DHS cannot provide any assurance that relief will be granted in all cases.").

[111] Individuals who do not meet these criteria could still request or be granted deferred action outside of DACA.

[112] See, e.g., Department of Homeland Security Appropriations Act, 2012, P.L. 112-74, Div. D., tit. ii, 125 Stat. 950 (Dec. 23, 2011) ("[T]he Secretary of Homeland Security shall prioritize the identification and removal of aliens convicted of a crime by the severity of that crime."); Department of Homeland Security Appropriations Act, 2010, P.L. 111-83, Div. D., tit. III, 123 Stat. 2142 (Oct. 28, 2009) (same); Department of Homeland Security Appropriations Act, P.L. 110-329, Div. D, tit. ii, 122 Stat. 3659 (Sept. 30, 2008) (same); Consolidated Appropriations Act, 2008, P.L. 110- 161, 121 Stat. 2050-51 (Dec. 26, 2007) (funding to "improve and modernize efforts to identify aliens convicted of a crime, sentenced to imprisonment, and who may be deportable, and remove them from the United States"); H.R. REPT. 111-157, at 6 (2009) ("[R]ather than simply rounding up as many illegal immigrants as possible, which is sometimes achieved by targeting the easiest and least threatening among the undocumented population, DHS must ensure that the government's huge investments in immigration enforcement are producing the maximum return in making our country safer.").

[113] See, e.g., Civil Immigration Enforcement, supra note 8, at 1-2 (aliens who have been convicted of crimes, are at least 16 years of age and participate in organized criminal gangs, are subject to outstanding criminal warrants, or "otherwise pose a serious risk to public safety" constituting the highest priorities for removal). Relatedly, Secretary Napolitano's announcement of the DACA initiative expressly excluded from consideration for deferred action under DACA persons who have been convicted of a felony, a "significant misdemeanor," or multiple misdemeanors. See Exercising Prosecutorial Discretion with Respect to Individuals Who Came to the United States as Children, supra note 10, at 1.

[114] Heckler, 470 U.S. at 832.

[115] 5 U.S.C. §701(a)(2). This presumption is an exception to the general rule that the APA "embodi[es] a 'basic presumption of judicial review.'" Lincoln v. Vigil, 508 U.S. 182, 190 (1993) (quoting Abbott Labs. v. Gardner, 387 U.S. 136, 140 (1967)).

[116] 470 U.S. at 832-33. See also id. at 833 ("[I]n establishing this presumption [of nonreviewability] in the APA, Congress did not set agencies free to disregard legislative direction in the statutory scheme that the agency administers. Congress may limit an agency's exercise of enforcement power if it wishes, either by setting substantive priorities, or by otherwise circumscribing an agency's power to discriminate among issues or cases it will pursue.").

[117] See, e.g., Arizona v. United States, No. 11-182, Amicus Curiae Brief of Secure States Initiative in Support of Petitioners, at 8-9; Crane, Amended Complaint, supra note 3, at ¶¶ 38-40.

[118] INA §235(a)(1), (a)(3), and (b)(2)(A); 8 U.S.C. §1225(a)(1), (a)(3), and (b)(2)(A).

[119] Crane, No. 3:12-cv-03247-O, 2013 U.S. Dist. LEXIS 57788, at *28-*29 (N.D. Tex., Apr. 23, 2013).

[120] Crane, Order, supra note 79.

[121] See, e.g., 8 C.F.R. §236.1(c) & (d); Matter of Oseiwusu, 22 I. & N. Dec. 19 (BIA 1998) ("According to the regulations, an Immigration Judge has no authority over the

apprehension, custody, and detention of arriving aliens and is therefore without authority to consider the bond request of an alien returning pursuant to a grant of advance parole.").

[122] See Arizona v. United States,—U.S.—132 S. Ct. 2492 (2012). Moreover, even if a reviewing court construed Section 235 of the INA as statutorily compelling DHS to place aliens who unlawfully entered the United States into removal proceedings, DHS would not necessarily be barred from exercising certain forms of prosecutorial discretion as to DACA beneficiaries after these individuals have been placed into removal proceedings. See generally Crane, Amended Complaint, supra 3, at ¶ 71 ("[A]ny 'prosecutorial discretion' that Defendants exercise must be consistent with 8 U.S.C. § 1225 and can only occur after an alien has been placed into removal proceedings as required by 8 U.S.C. §1225, or under a provision of federal law expressly authorizing such 'prosecutorial discretion.'").

[123] Arizona, 132 S. Ct. at 2499 ("A principal feature of the removal system is the broad discretion exercised by immigration officials. Federal officials, as an initial matter, must decide whether it makes sense to pursue removal at all. If removal proceedings commence, aliens may seek asylum and other discretionary relief allowing them to remain in the country or at least to leave without formal removal. Discretion in the enforcement of immigration law embraces immediate human concerns. ... Some discretionary decisions [also] involve policy choices that bear on this Nation's international relations. ... The dynamic nature of relations with other countries requires the Executive Branch to ensure that enforcement policies are consistent with this Nation's foreign policy with respect to these and other realities.") (internal citations omitted)).

[124] See, e.g., Lopez v. Davis, 531 U.S. 230, 241 (2001) ("Congress' use of the permissive 'may' in § 3621(e)(2)(B) contrasts with the legislators' use of a mandatory 'shall' in the very same section. Elsewhere in § 3621, Congress used 'shall' to impose discretionless obligations, including the obligation to provide drug treatment when funds are available. See 18 U.S.C. § 3621(e)(1) ('Bureau of Prisons shall, subject to the availability of appropriations, provide residential substance abuse treatment (and make arrangements for appropriate aftercare)'); see also, e.g., § 3621(b) ('The Bureau shall designate the place of the prisoner's imprisonment.... In designating the place of imprisonment or making transfers under this subsection, there shall be no favoritism given to prisoners of high social or economic status.'").

[125] INS and, later, DHS has also taken the position that the use of "shall" in a statute does not, by itself, limit the ability of immigration officers to exercise prosecutorial discretion, and the agencies' views could potentially be entitled to some deference, as discussed below. See, e.g., 2002 INS Guidance, supra note 2 ("[A] statute directing that the INS 'shall' remove removable aliens would not be construed by itself to limit prosecutorial discretion."); INS Exercise of Prosecutorial Discretion, supra note 15, at 8 (opining that any statutory limits on INS's prosecutorial discretion must be "clear and specific").

[126] 470 U.S. at 835 (quoting 21 U.S.C. §334(a)(1) (emphasis added)).

[127] Id. See also id. at 842 (Marshall, J., concurring) (indicating that the Food, Drug, and Cosmetics Act is "not a mandatory statute" and, thus, the Food and Drug Administration has "significant discretion" to choose which alleged violations to prosecute).

[128] Matter of E-R-M & L-R-M, 25 I. & N. Dec. 520, 523 (BIA 2011).

[129] Id. at 522.

[130] Dunlop v. Bachowski, 421 U.S. 560, 567 (1975) (also considering the legislative history and the "nature of the administrative action involved").

[131] Id. at 563.

[132] Id. at 570.

[133] 480 F.2d at 1162. See also id. at 1163 (noting that "[t]he Act sets forth two alternative courses of action by which enforcement may be effected").

[134] 467 U.S. 837 (1984).

[135] 467 U.S. at 842-43.

[136] Barnhart v. Walton, 535 U.S. 212, 217 (2002) (quoting Chevron, 467 U.S. at 842-43).

[137] Id. at 218 (quoting, in part, Chevron, 467 U.S. at 843).

[138] Specifically, the regulation implementing the third INA provision noted above—regarding the detention of aliens seeking admission—applies only to arriving aliens, not to aliens who entered without admission. See 8 C.F.R. §235.3(c) ("[A]ny arriving alien who appears to the inspecting officer to be inadmissible, and who is placed in removal proceedings pursuant to section 240 of the Act shall be detained in accordance with section 235(b) of the Act"). This has been the agency's interpretation of the provision since the initial final rule implementing this provision. See INS, Inspection and Expedited Removal of Aliens; Detention and Removal of Aliens; Conduct of Removal Proceedings; Asylum Procedures, 62 Fed. Reg. 10312, 10357 (Mar. 6, 1997) (codified at 8 C.F.R. §235.3(c)). See also INS, Inspection and Expedited Removal of Aliens; Detention and Removal of Aliens; Conduct of Removal Proceedings; Asylum Procedures, 62 Fed. Reg. 444, 444-46 (Jan. 3, 1997) (noting that the INA "distinguishes between the broader term 'applicants for admission' and a narrower group, 'arriving aliens'"). The term "arriving alien" is defined in the regulations as "an applicant for admission coming or attempting to come into the United States at a port-of-entry, or an alien seeking transit through the United States at a port-of-entry, or an alien interdicted in international or United States waters and brought into the United States," but does not include aliens who entered without inspection. See 8 C.F.R. §1.2.

[139] The position of DHS and DOJ may also reflect concerns that if Section 235(b)(2)(A) were construed to apply to all applicants for admission, the statutory language regarding "seeking admission" would be superfluous, and construing statutes so as to give effect to all of their provisions is one of the fundamental principles of statutory interpretation. See, e.g., Hibbs v. Winn, 542 U.S. 88, 101 (2004) ("A statute should be construed so that effect is given to all its provisions, so that no part will be inoperative or superfluous, void or insignificant."); Montclair v. Ramsdell, 107 U.S. 147, 152 (1883) (Courts should "give effect, if possible, to every clause and word of a statute, avoiding, if it may be, any construction which implies that the legislature was ignorant of the meaning of the language it employed."). Similarly, if detention were mandatory for all applicants for admission under INA 235(b)(2)(A), then the language including inadmissible aliens under the mandatory detention provision in Section 236(c)(1)(A) and (D) of the INA would arguably be superfluous as well, since the only aliens in the United States who are subject to the grounds of inadmissibility are applicants for admission. The agencies' interpretation does not appear to have been directly adopted by any court, although it arguably has been implicitly adopted in various court and BIA rulings that have applied a DHS regulation which provides that immigration judges have jurisdiction over bond determinations for aliens present without inspection, but not for arriving aliens. See, e.g., Matter of Oseiwusu, 22 I. & N. Dec. 19 (BIA 1998) ("According to the regulations, an Immigration Judge has no authority over the apprehension, custody, and detention of arriving aliens and is therefore without authority to consider the bond request of an alien returning pursuant to a grant of advance parole.").

[140] Crane, 2013 U.S. Dist. LEXIS 57788, at *23-*24.

[141] Id., at *25.

[142] See supra note 120 and accompanying text.

[143] INA §236(c)(1)-(2); 8 U.S.C. §1226(c)(1)-(2).

[144] See, e.g., 2002 INS Guidance, supra note 2, at 3 (indicating that detention pursuant to Section 236(c) is mandatory because Section 236(c) "evidences a specific congressional intention to limit discretion not to detain certain criminal aliens in removal proceedings that would otherwise exist"); INS Exercise of Prosecutorial Discretion, supra note 15, at 11. However, some commentators have noted that, notwithstanding this view, immigration agencies have released aliens subject to "mandatory detention" in order to moot lawsuits challenging the alien's detention. See, e.g., Stephen H. Legomsky, The Detention of Aliens: Theories, Rules, and Discretion, 30 U. MIAMI INTER-AM. L. REV. 531, 534 (1999).

[145] See, e.g., Pacific Molasses Co. v. Fed. Trade Comm'n, 356 F.2d 386, 389-90 (5th Cir. 1996) ("When an administrative agency promulgates rules to govern its proceedings, these rules must be scrupulously observed. This is so even when the defined procedures are '... generous beyond the requirements that bind such agency ...' For once an agency exercises its discretion and creates the procedural rules under which it desires to have its actions judged, it denies itself the right to violate these rules."). But see Farrell v. Dep't of the Interior, 314 F.3d 584, 590 (Fed. Cir. 2002) ("The general consensus is that an agency statement, not issued as a formal regulation, binds the agency only if the agency intended the statement to be binding.").

[146] Nicholas v. INS, 590 F.2d 802, 805 (1979).

[147] Id. at 807.

[148] Id.

[149] Id.

[150] See, e.g., Vergel v. INS, 536 F.2d 755, 757-80 (8th Cir. 1976) (upholding the deportation order, but staying its mandate for a period of time to allow the alien to apply for deferred action); David v. INS, 548 F.2d 219, 223 (8th Cir. 1977) (same); Yoon v. INS, 538 F.2d 1211, 1213 (5th Cir. 1976) (decision to grant or deny deferred action was within the "particular discretion of the INS," and the agency had the power to create and employ a category "for its own administrative convenience without standardizing the category and allowing applications for inclusion in it"); Lennon v. INS, 527 F.2d 187, 191 n.7 (2nd Cir. 1975) (describing deferred action as an "informal administrative stay of deportation").

[151] See, e.g., Leon Wildes, The Deferred Action Program of the Bureau of Citizenship and Immigration Services: A Possible Remedy for Impossible Immigration Cases, 41 SAN DIEGO L. REV. 819, 822 (2004).

[152] See, e.g., Charles Gordon, Stanley Mailman, & Stephen Yale-Loehr, IMMIGR. L. & PROC. §72.03(2)(h) n.120 (2009) (noting that the Operating Instruction addressing deferred action was rescinded in 1997).

[153] Community Nutrition Institute v. Young, 818 F.2d 943, 948 (1987) (finding that the FDA's thresholds for aflatoxins in corn were legislative rules that should have been promulgated through notice-and-comment rulemaking because the levels "have a present effect and are binding," and marketing any food not within the levels is viewed as unlawful). But see Heckler, 470 U.S. at 837 (rejecting a challenge to the Food and Drug Administration's refusal to enforce alleged violations of the Food, Drug, and Cosmetic Act, in part, because the agency "policy statement" in question did not "arise in the course of discussing the agency's discretion to exercise its enforcement power" and, thus, did not limit this discretion). The Court in Heckler expressly left open the possibility that certain agency rules might provide adequate guidelines for informed judicial review of decisions not to enforce them. Id. at 836.

[154] See, e.g., 2011 DHS Guidance, supra note 9, at 6.

[155] See, e.g., Columbia Broadcasting Sys., Inc. v. United States, 316 U.S. 407, 416 (1942) ("The particular label placed upon it by the Commission is not necessarily conclusive, for it is the substance of what the Commission has purported to do and has done which is decisive."); Guardian Fed. Savings & Loan Ass'n v. Fed. Savings & Loan Ins. Corp., 589 F.2d 658, 666-67 (D.C. Cir. 1978) ("If it appears that a so-called policy statement is in purpose or likely effect one that narrowly limits administrative discretion, it will be taken for what it is—a binding rule of substantive law."). The agency's characterization could, however, potentially be entitled to some deference. See, e.g., Community Nutrition Institute, 818 F.2d at 946.

[156] Crane v. Napolitano, No. 3:12-cv-03247-O, Brief in Support of Plaintiffs' Application for Preliminary Injunction, at 19 (filed N.D. Tex., Nov. 28, 2012). See also Crane v. Napolitano, No. 3:12-cv-03247-O, Affidavit of Christopher L. Crane, ¶ 8 (filed N.D. Tex., Nov. 27, 2012) (alleging that ICE has adopted a practice of not questioning individuals who assert that they could be eligible for deferred action as part of the DACA initiative, thereby effectively making all who claim deferred action entitled to it).

[157] See, e.g., Julia Preston, U.S. to Review Cases Seeking Deportations, New York Times, Nov. 17, 2011, available at http://www.nytimes.com/2011/11/17/us/deportation-cases-of-illegal-immigrants-to-be-reviewed.html.

[158] Rodriguez v. Holder, 668 F.3d 670 (9th Cir. 2012); Agustin v. Holder, 668 F.3d 672 (9th Cir. 2012); Jex v. Holder, 668 F.3d 673 (9th Cir. 2012); Pocasangre v. Holder, 668 F.3d 674 (9th Cir. 2012); Mata-Fasardo v. Holder, 668 F.3d 674 (9th Cir. 2012).

[159] Agustin, 668 F.3d at 672 (O'Scannlain, J., dissenting).

[160] Id. Subsequently, in response to the DACA initiative, the U.S. Court of Appeals for the Second Circuit ("Second Circuit") established a procedure whereby pending immigration cases are tolled while the government determines whether to remand the case to the BIA for administrative closure in light of DACA and related initiatives. In Matter of Immigration Petitions for Review Pending in the United States Court of Appeals for the Second Circuit, No. 12-4096, 2012 U.S. App. LEXIS 21555 (Oct. 16, 2012). However, unlike the Ninth Circuit, the Second Circuit did not order ICE to inform it regarding whether ICE plans to exercise discretion in particular cases.

[161] See supra note 12 and accompanying text.

[162] See, e.g., Durbin Statement on DREAM Act and Administrative Action to Help Young Immigrants, June 15, 2012, available at http://durbin.senate.gov/public/index.cfm/pressreleases?ID=070d1061-66c4-45ef-bb34-41da7e1e7d40.

[163] See, e.g., Pelosi, Nadler, Honda, and 81 Members of Congress Urge Department of Homeland Security Again To Recognize LGBT Family Ties in Deportation Cases, (copy on file with the authors).The need for discretion in certain cases involving aliens in same-sex marriages may have been removed by DHS's response to the recent Supreme Court decision in United States v. Windsor. Windsor struck down Section 3 of the Defense of Marriage Act (DOMA), which had precluded federal agencies from recognizing same-sex marriages. Following this decision, DHS began permitting U.S. citizens and lawful permanent residents to sponsor their same-sex spouses for family-based immigrant visas and adjustment of status. See DHS, Implementation of the Supreme Court Ruling on the Defense of Marriage Act, available at http://www.dhs.gov/topic/implementation-supreme-court-ruling-defense-marriage-act.

[164] Hinder the Administration's Legalization Temptation (HALT) Act, H.R. 2497, §2(f), 113th Cong. (permitting the grant of deferred action or extended voluntary departure only for the purpose of maintaining an alien in the United States "(1) to be tried for a crime, or to be a

witness at trial, upon the request of a Federal, State, or local law enforcement agency; (2) for any other significant law enforcement or national security purpose; or (3) for a humanitarian purpose where the life of the alien is imminently threatened").

165 Prohibiting the Back-Door Amnesty Act, H.R. 5953, §2(a), 113th Cong. ("nullifying" the 2011 Morton memoranda and the 2012 Napolitano memorandum).

166 See Heckler, 470 U.S. at 833 ("... Congress did not set agencies free to disregard legislative direction in the statutory scheme that the agency administers. Congress may limit an agency's exercise of enforcement power if it wishes, either by setting substantive priorities, or by otherwise circumscribing an agency's power to discriminate among issues or cases it will pursue.").

167 Adams, 480 F.2d at 1162.

168 Heckler, 470 U.S. at 832.

169 Chevron, 467 U.S. at 842-43.

170 See U.S. Const., art. I, §9, cl. 7 ("No Money shall be drawn from the Treasury, but in Consequence of Appropriations made by Law.... ").

171 See, e.g., Department of Homeland Security Appropriations Act, 2013, H.R. 5855, as passed by the House, §581(a), 113th Cong. ("None of the funds made available in this Act may be used to finalize, implement, administer, or enforce the 'Morton Memos.'").

INDEX

D

E

F

G

H

I

R

S

T

U

V

W

Y